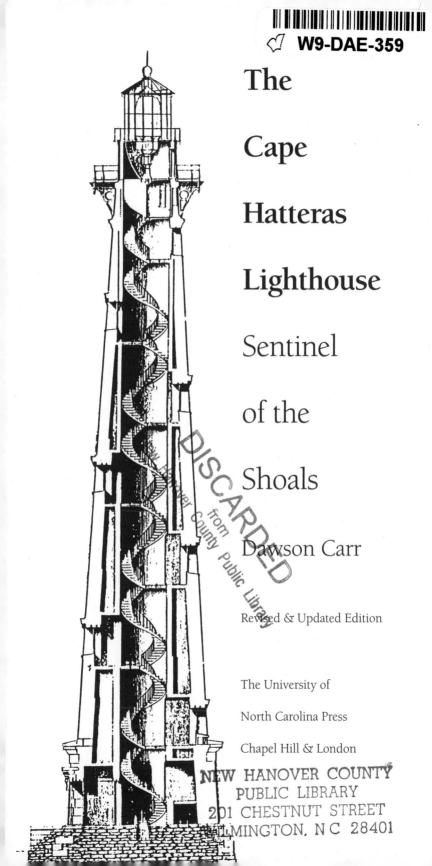

The

Cape

Hatteras

Lighthouse

Sentinel

of the

Shoals

Dawson Carr

Revised & Updated Edition

The University of

North Carolina Press

Chapel Hill & London

© 1991, 2000
The University
of North Carolina
Press
All rights reserved

Manufactured
in the United States
of America

The paper in this
book meets the
guidelines for
permanence and
durability of the
Committee on
Production
Guidelines for
Book Longevity
of the Council
on Library
Resources.

04 03 02 01 00
5 4 3 2 1

Library of Congress
Cataloging-in-Publication
Data

Carr, Dawson.
The Cape Hatteras lighthouse:
sentinel of the shoals / Dawson
Carr.—Rev. and upd. ed.
    p.   cm.
Includes bibliographical
references and index.
ISBN 0-8078-4876-X
(pbk.: alk. paper)
1. Cape Hatteras Lighthouse (N.C.)
I. Title.
VK1025.C27 C37   2000
387.1'55'09756175—dc21
99-089872

The

Cape

Hatteras

Lighthouse

To my wife,

Bobbie,

and my children,

Larry, Becky,

Scott, & Greg,

who have

brightened my way

through life's

shoals

Contents

Illustrations

Preface

Perhaps no facet of U.S. history is as fascinating and appealing to citizens of this country as the chronicles of its lighthouses. The tall and majestic structures that guard the lonely coastlines evoke a rare enchantment that links us to our maritime past, stirring awe and respect for the accomplishments of our ancestors.

Lighthouses usually were situated to mark harbors or hazardous regions of the coast, and thus they served either to guide or to caution, depending on the location. Placed where they were most needed, the lighthouses were often built in remote locations—desolate sites where construction was difficult and where the keepers observed lonely vigils, visited only by birds and the occasional supply boat. The bleak, friendless coasts required the lighthouse keepers to exercise great diligence amidst their solitary existences, yet many thrived in that environment and faithfully kept the lights burning despite all hardships.

Towering above sandy beaches where weathered, stunted trees might provide the only other break in the flatness of the landscape, these lighthouses were imposing and magnificent. Although primarily functional in design, they were often embellished with ornate ironwork and distinctive paint schemes that lent each one a special appeal. But it was the quality of their lanterns, rather than their charm, that supplied their main reason for being. A light that could not be seen from many miles offshore was worse than no light at all, for once a ship came too close to shore and found itself among the shoals, it had little hope of salvation. Therefore, lighthouses needed strong lamps able to project their beams farther than a dozen miles. The invention of the Fresnel lens in the early nineteenth century greatly enhanced the power of lighthouse lamps, and a beacon with a first-order Fresnel lens, the largest type, could be spotted up to twenty miles away.

All lighthouses must be tall enough to stand above the surrounding dunes and to provide a sufficiently high focal plane for their lanterns, but they come in varying sizes according to their designated roles. Channel lighthouses that mark inlets usually stand less than 100 feet high, but coastal lighthouses designed to warn of obstacles extending far out from shore might reach upward 150 feet or more.

Time and technology have gradually rendered lighthouses less essential; even as the lighthouses themselves improved, the need for them diminished. Ships with diesel engines no longer have to depend on the vagaries of fickle winds, and radar allows them to bypass any storms. Global positioning systems based on satellite signals can help navigators determine the location of their ships with great accuracy, and sonar can easily determine the depth of the water under the keel. Yet many small craft still depend on lighthouses, and recognition of the coded pattern of blinks from a distant beacon can be comforting to sailors aboard larger ships who still have qualms about total reliance on instruments.

In spite of the lighthouses' dwindling role, many still stand along the eastern coastline of the United States. Their spotty but strategic placement assures that the most dangerous zones of the seacoast between Maine and Florida remain safe for shipping. The majority of surviving lighthouses date from earlier centuries, but many are still operational.

Six working lighthouses can be found along the long, meandering coast of North Carolina. From the Oak Island light, the southernmost lighthouse in the state and the brightest in America, to Currituck Beach lighthouse near Corolla, perhaps none is better known or more popular than the Cape Hatteras lighthouse. At more than two hundred feet high, it is the tallest lighthouse in America and has stood near the point at Cape Hatteras since shortly after the Civil War.

The Cape Hatteras lighthouse was built to warn ships away from Diamond Shoals, the most hazardous part of the region some have labeled the Graveyard of the Atlantic. It is a scary place, in which major shipping lanes, merging warm and cold currents, and shifting underwater shoals converge with disastrous results, and it is known worldwide for its perils. Often shrouded in fog and mist, the low trees and dunes of Hatteras Island offer few visual landmarks to warn crews of their proximity to the shoals, and ships can slip all too easily into the shallows. Barnacle-encrusted skeletons of wrecked ships still rest there, attesting to the fact that, once trapped, there is little chance of escape.

The location of the Cape Hatteras lighthouse on North Carolina's legendary Outer Banks has made the structure one of the most recognized and visited lighthouses in America. It has a long and interesting history that includes the record of its own escape from the threat of encroaching waters, a narrative of human achievement in the eternal battle with the sea. This book tells the story of that colorful past, including the incredible account of the successful efforts to rescue the fabled Cape Hatteras lighthouse from almost certain destruction.

Acknowledgments

Writing a book about North Carolina's Outer Banks has been a fascinating project because of the area's adventure-rich history, and I owe thanks to the many interesting people who have helped me directly or indirectly. David Stick's excellent, well-researched books about the Outer Banks have set the standard for literature on that region and have guided me in separating fact from fiction in my own research. I also am indebted to Ross Holland Jr. for his detailed descriptions of the Cape Hatteras lighthouse and for his technical assistance in labeling its architectural features.

Several members of the National Park Service have helped, including Warren Wrenn, Penny Ambrose, and Bebe Woody, who provided assistance in locating information and photographs for inclusion in this book. Also, Steve Harrison at Cape Hatteras supplied specific, reliable data on the lighthouse and the relocation project when information from other sources proved conflicting.

The professional staffs of the North Carolina Collection in Chapel Hill and the North Carolina Division of Archives and History in Raleigh were patient and helpful. Richard Jones, publisher of the *Hatteras Monitor*, gave me many good suggestions.

I owe particular thanks to Mike Booher, who provided many of the contemporary photographs used in the book, including aerial and ground views from his comprehensive photographic record of the relocation project, much of which can be seen in his forthcoming book, *Out of Harm's Way*. Bruce Roberts and Cheryl Shelton-Roberts of the Outer Banks Lighthouse Society provided issues of the quarterly publication *Lighthouse News* and a copy of their excellent booklet, *Moving Hatteras: Relocating the Cape Hatteras Light Station to Safety*.

This book would not have been complete without information garnered from personal interviews with three people: Hugh Morton, one of North Carolina's leading promoters and organizer of the Save the Lighthouse Committee; Rany Jennette, son of the last keeper of the Cape Hatteras lighthouse; and David Fischetti, a Cary engineer who helped form the Move the Lighthouse Committee. Each related personal experiences and details that could not be found in any printed source. David provided names of individuals and companies involved in moving the lighthouse, explained some of the processes, and offered diagrams to clarify the mechanics of the operation.

Many members of the faculty and staff at Sandhills Community College helped me, including Richard Lewis Jr., Nancy Rountree, Tim Swenson, and Teresa Wood. The staff of the Sandhills library procured hard-to-get materials through the interlibrary loan system. Stephen Smith, professor of English and columnist for the Southern Pines newspaper, *The Pilot*, read and corrected my various drafts. Annette Blue, Wayne Burris, and Carlene Dennison offered helpful suggestions.

Reynold Davenport redrew diagrams from the original lighthouse plans and helped secure engineering details about the relocation project. Joe Jakubik of the International Chimney Corporation helped clear up confusion about some details of the move, including the correct weight of the lighthouse.

I believe I would be derelict not to acknowledge the contributions of those responsible for saving the lighthouse. Without their efforts, there might have been no subject for this book left. The engineers and contractors who accomplished the move and the personnel of the National Park Service who pursued the project despite all opposition have my thanks. But it was Hugh Morton who formed the Save the Lighthouse Committee that first gained public support for the effort, and David Fischetti, Orrin Pilkey Jr., David Bush, and others of the Move the Lighthouse Committee who presented a workable plan to move the lighthouse almost twenty years ago. State senator Marc Basnight, U.S. Senator Lauch Faircloth, Governor Jim Hunt, and President Bill Clinton all helped salvage funding for the project at the eleventh hour, resulting in the rescue of both the legislation and the lighthouse itself.

I, like many others, would have liked to see the lighthouse remain where it was built, but encroachment by the Atlantic Ocean made that prospect unlikely. The relocation of the Cape Hatteras lighthouse to higher and safer ground has saved a major monument to our coastal heritage and one of our most important national treasures. Those who made it possible, and the many who helped me tell the story in this book, share my gratitude.

The

Cape

Hatteras

Lighthouse

1

Lighthouses

and

Shipwreck

The breakers were right beneath her bows,
*   She drifted a dreary wreck,*
And a whooping billow swept the crew
*   Like icicles from her deck.*

She struck where the white and fleecy waves
*   Looked soft as carded wool,*
But the cruel rocks, they gored her side
*   Like the horns of an angry bull.*

Her rattling shrouds, all sheathed in ice,
*   With the masts went by the board;*
Like a vessel of glass, she stove and sank,
*   Ho! Ho! the breakers roared!*

—Longfellow, "The Wreck of the Hesperus*"*

The proud schooner left New York on Saturday, 1 December 1812, under a favorable wind and sunny skies. Her sails billowed and snapped gently in the steady breeze, and the sea hissed by her bow as she slipped easily through calm waters.

On board was a Mrs. Harris of Hillsboro, N.C., who was heading home from New York with her younger sister Lydia. The trip ahead was especially exciting, for it held an element of danger. To reach the port of New Bern, North Carolina, they would have to sail southward for three hundred miles and then thread their way around perilous Diamond Shoals to enter Ocracoke Inlet. The seas there bore a tragic history of shipwreck, and the stormy season was at hand. Mrs. Harris's passage to New York had been pleasant, though, and she determined to keep a diary of the return trip to provide herself with a reminder of what she hoped would be a pleasant voyage.

For two days, the sailing was brisk and uneventful. She and her sister often rode topside, where they enjoyed the gentle wind and marveled at the gulls that soared behind the ship and swooped suddenly to the ocean's surface in search of food. It was Monday, 3 December, when they awoke to see the morning sky tinted red and splotched with low-lying, purplish clouds. Mrs. Harris knew that this was a bad omen for sailors, and she was filled with a sense of uneasiness. Her fears were soon realized, for both the weather and the voyage rapidly took a turn for the worse. Mrs. Harris recounted in her diary: "The wind shifted round, and from that hour severe gales, head-winds, and dead calm alternated. Much did we suffer. I think I was more dreadfully sick than on any former voyage."

Lydia was seasick for only a few hours, but Mrs. Harris's illness continued for four days. One week after they departed New York, a tremendous gale struck the ship, placing the craft in danger of foundering and filling Mrs. Harris with fears for herself and Lydia. "The wind blew so violently that we were driven at the rate of ten miles an hour toward The Hook without a single sail up. It thundered tremendously, and as I lay in my berth I saw the vivid flashes of lightning playing over the companionway. Rain, hail, and snow succeeded each other, and had not a kind Providence endowed our captain with great firmness and presence of mind in a critical moment we must all have been lost. I felt we were in great danger; I pressed our darling Lydia to my bosom and exclaimed, 'Oh, that I had left you at home!'"

Severe gales continued to batter the ship as it attempted to pass through Ocracoke Inlet and reach the town of New Bern. Each time the ship was about to "cross the bar," headwinds forced the vessel back into the Gulf Stream. "Sixteen days and nights we lay in that dangerous place," she said. "Our wood gave out, provisions grew short, and the patience of the crew was nearly exhausted."

On 23 December, the weather worsened and a vicious storm struck the ship, threatening to force it onto the dreaded shoals at Cape Hatteras. The captain spent hours on the deck, peering fearfully through the haze, hoping to glimpse the lighthouse that marked the proximity of the shoals he knew could not be far away. The weather was so dreadful that even the first mate, the captain's younger brother, was too sick to rise from his berth. A crewman who continued to heave the lead to determine the depth of the ocean soon discovered they were in the shallows. With the wind blowing directly toward shore, the captain decided he must turn about and head for the relative safety of the open sea. "Captain Pike justly deemed it dangerous to proceed further towards the Cape or to lie there."

When they found themselves in deep water, the vessel was laid to. "All danger, we thought, was over, and we lay quietly down to sleep. Alas! we are often in the greatest danger when we think ourselves most secure!" When the wind changed direction suddenly just before daylight, it "raised heavy opposite seas, and so strong was the current that it drove us with irresistible violence towards the shore." The torrential rains and stormy skies obscured any glimpse of the Cape Hatteras light, but the presence of the shallows seemed to indicate they were in the midst of Diamond Shoals, the most feared location on the eastern coast of the United States.

Around five o'clock on Christmas Eve morning, while still shrouded in a darkness brightened only by intermittent flashes of lightning, the ship lurched against the sandy bottom, waking Mrs. Harris. "In an instant we were all out of our berths; the captain flew on deck, the vessel began to fill with water and inclined much on one side, which was soon overflown. Down the stairs rushed the captain, exclaiming, 'By the eternal God, we're on the breakers!' Oh, what a sound was that!" All those on board trembled with fear as the craft wallowed at the mercy of the thrashing waves, and loose objects were flung about the interior, narrowly missing several of the passengers. "Shrieks of anguish resounded through the vessel," wrote Mrs. Harris. "It thumped violently on the breakers, and in a few moments was turned over nearly on its beam ends. . . . The gentlemen stood around like statues of despair, deeming all efforts to save themselves or us useless. Mr. Davis held my hand with one of his, with the other he held a candle, when a heavy sea broke over the vessel, shivered the skylight to atoms, rushed into the cabin and extinguished the light. The cabin was nearly filled with water."

The women passengers were brought into Mrs. Harris's cabin, where they continuously cried out their prayers for salvation. When the male passengers went on deck to determine the status of the ship, they discovered they were not on the shoals, as they had thought, but instead were stranded nearly on the beach. According to Mrs. Harris, "The breakers ran too high to permit them to swing ashore, and the long-boat had long ago burst from its holdings and floated off. All they could do, therefore, was to cling to the shrouds though almost dead with the intense cold, in the feeble hope that our situation might be discovered and we receive assistance."

After the men had gone on deck, a mighty wave swept over the ship and roared down the stairs into the cabin where the women waited. It flooded the interior and pushed aside everything in its path. "All communication with those on deck seemed now cut off; heavy seas were constantly rushing in upon us and we all thought ourselves drowning. Miss Henry rushed past me exclaiming, 'O, Mrs. Harris, do not let us stay here and be drowned; let us try to get on deck!' She went to the skylight, put her hand through the broken bars and screamed most piteously for help." Another tremendous wave washed over the vessel and threw Miss Henry on her back. "Not a sound was heard by us from the deck, so loud and awfully roared the breakers, and I verily thought that the captain, sailors and passengers had all been swept overboard. I thought we were all alone in the shattered vessel, and at such a distance from any human beings that we could not be descried."

The miserable little group huddled together to pray, but their faith was shaken as the heaviest sea yet exploded upon the vessel, filling their mouths and noses with salty water and nearly drowning them all.

We then sat in awful stupefaction awaiting death, but . . . it was death in such an awful form! I looked out at the door—naught could be seen but the awful breakers rolling over the remains of the vessel and smoking like a vast building in flames. The cabin was several feet deep in water, on which were floating trunks, baskets, mattresses and bedding. Crash! crash! went the broken vessel continually. The hold broke open with violence, and boxes, barrels, etc., were bursting out. The berth in which we sat began filling with water; the planks beneath our feet began to separate, displaying the roaring waves, which seemed gaping to swallow us.

Unknown to those below decks, the ship gradually had been washed nearer the beach by the force of the surf, and when the waves ebbed, residents of Hatteras Island had rushed out and plucked people from the stranded vessel until all but one of those on deck had been rescued. Unfortunately, the captain's brother tried desperately to swim ashore but, due to his weakened physical condition, was unable to survive the surging, powerful waves. He drowned before those on shore could reach him. The captain quickly told them of the women trapped in the cabin and pleaded that they be saved. A slave of one of the residents was asked if he would be willing to attempt the rescue, and he immediately consented.

On board the women waited, lamenting their fate. Suddenly, one of them exclaimed that someone was coming to their rescue, but no one believed her.

> I thought she was deceiving herself, and trembled for her mistake; but in an instant a large, intrepid Negro was seen by us all making his way over the scattered remnants of the vessel to our room—quickly passed on discovering that we were alive (which he had not expected), and made up to the dead-lights, which with wonderful strength, he pushed out with his arm (although they had withstood the force of so many waves), and then handed Miss Hines, Miss Henry, Lydia, myself and the remaining servant out of the cabin window to some men who stood on the beach to receive us. . . .
>
> We were taken with our wet night-clothes on and nearly perished with cold . . . to a miserable little hut about a mile from the shore. When Captain Pike met Lydia he burst into tears, overjoyed at learning we were all alive; never, he says, did he experience greater satisfaction. The inmates of the wretched dwelling to which we were carried prepared some food for us, but my heart was too full to permit me to eat.

The miserable condition in which they found themselves was quickly forgotten; at least they were alive. If they had ended up on Diamond Shoals, miles from the helpful reach of those on shore, there would have been little hope of survival. Only a mile downshore, another vessel had struck an hour earlier, when the storm was at its worst and the tide at its maximum. This unfortunate vessel had been smashed and its entire crew had perished. "Had we been on the shores of Cape Hatteras (as we at first thought), doubtless we should all have perished, but we struck on the shore eight miles north of the Cape."

Mrs. Harris and the other passengers lamented the loss of their trunks and other valuable articles, and they expressed dismay that the islanders who had rescued them seemed so avaricious. "Exulting in the calamity which has thrown us among them, though pretending to sympathize in our distress, they would steal the wet clothes which we took from our backs and hung out to dry, and everything belonging to us which they could lay their hands on." None of the rescued party understood that salvage was viewed as a legitimate activity by the island's residents, who readily risked their own lives to save those who otherwise would be left to the mercy of the sea and shared with them their meager food and "wretched dwellings." Is there anyone who would not quickly trade all earthly possessions in return for being rescued when a terrible death by drowning appears imminent and all hope seems lost? Thanks to the valiant efforts of those who lived in the shadow of the Cape Hatteras lighthouse, Mrs. Harris and the other passengers and crew, with the exception of the unfortunate first mate, were able to leave the island by boat and continue with their lives.

Safeguarding the Seas

Since the first intrepid voyager rode a hollowed-out log down a river, humans have sought to extend their ability to navigate the waters of the earth. Sails added power to later vessels, and only the vagaries of the wind bounded the ever-widening horizon as sailors ventured further away from land. As they steered boldly out onto the ocean, land faded to a smudge on the horizon and eventually disappeared. Knowledge of the stars and trust in astrolabe and compass gave the voyagers their only assurance that home port could be found again.

Storms easily drove ships from their courses and pushed

Debris from a ship wrecked on the Outer Banks. Salvage was viewed as a legitimate activity by those who lived on Hatteras Island, and they frequently recovered cargo and timbers that had washed ashore from storm-battered ships unfortunate enough to be caught near Diamond Shoals. (Courtesy of the U.S. National Park Service)

them toward unknown dangers. Even known ports were often flanked by treacherous rocks or shallows that threatened to rip open the wooden hulls of the stoutest sailing craft. Sailors feared the land more than the sea, for it was land that threatened to smash them and their ships or strand them irretrievably, far from home, on some distant shoal. Many mothers, wives, and children waited in vain for the return of loved ones who sailed away on a ship, never to return.

The first beacons to mark the way for sailors were bonfires placed on seaside hilltops by the anxious families of those who chose to "go down to the sea in ships." How reassuring that small column of smoke or faint glow of the flame must have been to travelers who had sailed for days on the empty, monotonous seas devoid of familiar landmarks. The higher the hilltop, the farther the tiny flames could be seen, so it was a natural step in the evolution of beacons to increase their reach by using towers to hold the signal fires aloft. Thus was born the concept of a lighthouse.

Warning of navigational hazards was as important as marking the home port, for ships whose hulls were crushed by rock-bound coasts or pounded to bits by breakers in shoal-lined waters had no need of beacons to guide their return. The Vikings, Phoenicians, and Romans all took an early interest in marking safe passageways for seafarers, and they placed many signal lights to guide them homeward and away from treacherous areas.

One area where ancient commerce flourished was the cradle of civilization that surrounded the Mediterranean Sea. Trade among the Egyptians, Romans, and Greeks depended on sea travel, and Alexandria, Egypt, became a port of great importance. It was there that one of the most famous lighthouses of all time, the Tower of Pharos, was constructed. Listed as one of the Seven Wonders of the Ancient World, the tower was designed by Sostros and built under the authority of Ptolemy II in 261 B.C. It took nineteen years to complete, reached a towering 450 feet, and had a signal fire that could be seen for almost thirty miles. No other lighthouse in history was so tall or endured so long. Fifteen centuries later, wood was still being carried daily to the giant brazier at the top, providing flames for guidance by night and a column of smoke to be seen by day. Wood was scarce in the area, and it must have been a massive undertaking to provide fuel for that beacon every day for fifteen hundred years. That the lighthouse was kept in operation for so long, in spite of the scarcity of fuel and the many wars fought near it, underscores its importance. The Arabian geographer Edrisi found that the marble tower was still in excellent condition when he examined it in the thirteenth century, but later that same century it was devastated by an earthquake.

Through the ages, many lighthouses were known by those who plied the seas. Infamous through their association with the hazardous areas they marked, their names struck fear into the

The Tower of Pharos. One of the Seven Wonders of the Ancient World, it guided ships into the harbor at Alexandria, Egypt, for nearly fifteen hundred years before it was finally felled by an earthquake in the thirteenth century A.D. At 450 feet, it was the world's tallest lighthouse. From John Harris, Complete Collection of Voyages and Travels, *1744. (Courtesy of the Rare Book Room, Perkins Library, Duke University, Durham, N.C.)*

hearts of mariners forced to pass close to such forbidding places as Eddystone, Coffin Island, Wolf Rock, and Danger Point. But the warnings from lights and foghorns provided the only hope for sailors whose unreliable maps and inaccurate instruments left the exact location of rock and reef as hazy as the fog that often obscured their way.

The Romans, who depended on sea traffic to maintain their vast, far-flung empire, had as many as thirty lighthouses in operation by the fifth century A.D. But after the empire had fallen to invading barbarians, the practice of using beacons to lure ships onto the reefs, rather than to warn them off, became widespread. This misuse of lighthouses led to many ships being wrecked and ravaged by pirates. With their original purpose defeated, the signal towers were closed down. Thus the Dark Ages that descended upon Europe brought with them an accompanying blackness that obscured the reassuring glow of lighthouses there for centuries to come.

Gradually the maritime nations of Europe renewed their interest in sea travel and exploration. As ships again set forth in increasing numbers, the need for lighthouses once more became apparent, causing many of the old towers to be put back into operation and stimulating the construction of new ones. Because of the earlier misuses of signal fires, it became the custom, when lighthouse operations were restored, to entrust only holy men such as monks as their keepers.

By the sixteenth century, sea lights and markers had become increasingly important as trade flourished and travel to the New World expanded. Governments began to assume responsibility for building lighthouses and paid for their maintenance with tolls exacted from passing ships. The growing frequency of voyages to America as Spain, France, Portugal, and England established colonies there led also to increasing numbers of shipwrecks, but despite the tragic losses in lives and cargo, the colonizers showed little interest in constructing lighthouses along the coastlines of America.

One place in Colonial America where ships were frequently

lost was the region off the eastern coast of North Carolina. There, intersecting warm and cold currents combined with submerged shoals to form one of the worst traps for ships found anywhere in the world. The area quickly became notorious among mariners and was feared by all who traversed its stormy seas. The location at Cape Hatteras, North Carolina, was called Diamond Shoals, but it later acquired a more terrifying label, the Graveyard of the Atlantic. As vessel after vessel went down to lie entombed on the sandy bottom, ships' captains pleaded for a lighthouse to be placed there, but it was more than two hundred years after the first attempt to place an English colony on North Carolina's shores before a lighthouse was built on Hatteras Island to mark its treacherous shoals.

2

Early History of North Carolina's Outer Banks

The Outer Banks of North Carolina are a broken string of narrow islands that stretch for nearly two hundred miles from the Virginia border south to Morehead City. The barrier islands curve eastward like a scrawny arm embracing the mainland of North Carolina, with the elbow jutting out belligerently into the Atlantic at Cape Hatteras. The miles of white sandy dunes and scrub-covered lowlands bear the brunt of the severe storms that batter the area, sparing the mainland coast but suffering mutilation in the process. The slim strip of sand is only a mile across at places, and when winds force the water back into the sounds, it piles up and flows over the Banks to the sea, threatening to wash channels where none have existed.

Caught in the confluence of the icy Labrador Current, which brings cold blue water down from the frozen seas near Greenland, and the warm Gulf Stream as it sweeps northward in a long, curving arc from the tropics, the islands are buffeted frequently by angry waves. The eastern projection of the barrier islands into the Atlantic exposes them to hurricanes and wind-generated waves that can travel unimpeded for over two thousand miles before striking the shore. The spume sprayed into the air as waves hit the beach is carried far inland by winds and distorts the indigenous trees and shrubs into misshapen, grotesque forms. For a distance of about a quarter-mile from the surf, only the most salt-resistant plants survive. The beaches and dunes are bare except for sparse patches of sea oats and wax myrtles that cling tenuously to the loose sand.

For centuries Hatteras Island, the longest and easternmost segment of the Outer Banks, could only be reached by boat or ship, and its inaccessibility helped preserve its pristine beauty. The natural wildness of the region, where thousands of migratory birds gather in the late fall and uncluttered white beaches with undulating dunes stretch for miles, attracts over two-and-a-half million visitors each year. The Cape Hatteras region was the first to be designated a national seashore recreation area by the federal government, and today only a few small, isolated towns dot its miles of unspoiled wilderness. After the last tourist has packed up and disappeared, a few hardy residents remain in picturesque villages like Rodanthe or Buxton to savor the stormy loneliness of the Banks in winter.

Life is not always idyllic there, for it is a desolate area where winds can blow the sand with such force that it strips the paint from houses, and where the storms are so vicious they can open new inlets from sound to sea or close others. Windows are often frosted to opaqueness by the constant bombardment from millions of grains of sand hurled across the dunes by the wind. Salt spray from the pounding surf drifts over the narrow island,

Timbers of a shipwreck emerge from the sand on Hatteras Island. The shifting sands of the Outer Banks frequently reveal, then cover again, the ribs of some of the hundreds of vessels lost in this region of the Atlantic. (Photograph by Mike Booher)

seeking out iron to color it red with rust and causing hinges to creak hoarsely in protest. Storms called "nor'easters" swoop down in winter and spring to rival hurricanes in their sudden and destructive fury, threatening to tear houses from their uncertain moorings and alternately washing out the only road or concealing it with piles of drifted sand.

The entire length of the Outer Banks has been littered with the wreckage of ships thrust upon them mercilessly by storms and currents throughout the centuries. Bleached ribs and timbers of long-lost, often unknown derelicts are frequently exposed on shore when the sand shifts under the force of wind and tide. The weathered and barnacle-encrusted planks of forgotten vessels appear as if by magic, only to disappear again the next day. The bodies of so many unfortunate sailors have washed ashore after the destruction of their ships that the northern stretch of beach above Hatteras Island is still called Bodie (Body) Island.

The region has suffered many tragedies. The strategic location of the Banks made them a battleground during several wars, and human conflict joined natural disasters in lining the shoals with the remains of ships and men. Pirates were attracted by the available hiding places for their ships in the inlets and coves that bordered the sounds and estuaries and by the heavily traveled shipping lanes that ran just a few miles offshore. During the early eighteenth century, pirate raids occurred so frequently around Hatteras and Ocracoke islands that the period became known as the "golden age of piracy."

The exposed position of the Banks leaves them open to the full force of the elements, and living there requires the residents to adapt to nature in its purest form. This is a place where land, sea, and sky seem to touch. On the headlands at Cape Point, the candy-striped lighthouse blinks its coded warning of the presence of Diamond Shoals to all who dare pass.

Geological History of the Region

No one knows how long humans have lived on the Outer Banks, but when the first European colonists arrived on North Carolina's shores over four hundred years ago, the Algonquins who met them had already been there at least a thousand years. Yet, in terms of geological time, even that period represents the mere blink of an eye.

A few million years ago, the rolling Appalachian Mountains were taller, and they still showed the angular, irregular faces of broken rock formed by the buckling and uplifting of the earth's crust. Through countless eons, wind, rain, and temperature have weathered the hills and valleys of North Carolina. Erosion has worn down the jagged mountains like roaring streams wear smooth the rocks in their paths, and the residue of that erosion has washed down the rivers and into the sea, where it has settled gently but steadily to carpet the continental shelf.

At intervals of thousands of years, sea level has risen and fallen significantly as climatic changes caused the ice caps at the North and South poles to shrink or enlarge. As these ice ages come and go, they dramatically affect the earth's geography and weather and the survival of numerous species. At the peak of an ice age, large quantities of ocean water freeze into ice caps that cover much of the continental land mass, and huge glaciers push toward the equator. This glaciation is accompanied by a lowering of sea level around the world.

At the end of one of these cycles, ice caps melt and water returns to the ocean basins, causing sea level to rise again. Scientists believe that the rising waters form the accumulated silt and sediment on the continental shelf into a ridge. The sandy reef snowballs as it is pushed along by the expanding ocean. Rolled over and over by the continuing rise in water level, like clay before a bulldozer, this sandy strip drives the water of estuary and sound ahead of it and eventually forms a reef that separates the sea from the inland waters.

Evidence indicates that North Carolina's present barrier island formation is not new to the state but is only the latest in a series of similar features that have existed, then vanished, through the ages. To geologists, the sediment layers in North Carolina's coastal plain are like pages of a book, allowing them to read the history of the region's formation. Vestiges of several earlier barrier islands can be seen parallel to those of today, stretching north to south and extending westward in echelons almost as far west as Raleigh. Apparently North Carolina's Outer Banks live, die, and live again, Phoenix-like, as the climate changes. While they exist, they are dynamic, constantly shifting and moving westward as sea level rises.

The last ice age, known as the Wisconsin Glaciation period, began its decline about 18,000 years ago. In the 180 centuries since then, the level of the sea has risen perhaps as much as one hundred feet. Scientific estimates of the increase in sea level indicate a rise of six to twelve inches per century, but the rate has increased dramatically during the past twenty-five years, raising concerns about the so-called greenhouse effect. The sudden rise in the level of the ocean has been accompanied by accelerated movement and relocation of sand on the Outer

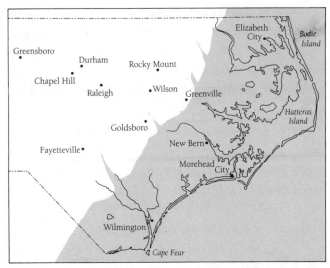

Approximate North Carolina shoreline forty-five million years ago. The Castle Hayne formation, one of four sediment formations that mark the North Carolina coastal plain, shows that the Atlantic Ocean once reached far inland from its present position. (Courtesy of Kathy Hart, University of North Carolina Sea Grant College Program)

Banks, causing worry among property owners, for even without significant flooding, erosion of the beaches could destroy many buildings there.

Outer Banks sand is composed largely of quartz and feldspar, but one part in four of Hatteras sand is made up of pulverized, bleached sea-animal skeletons. This composition gives the dunes the appearance of carved ivory sculpted by the wind. Light makes the minute particles sparkle and tints them with color at sunrise and sunset.

As the reef evolved, seeds were distributed over the dunes by wind and birds. Cedars, hollies, live oaks, grapevines, and grasses thrust their roots deeply into its soft, yielding surface. Plant growth stabilized the shifting sands and acted as a seine to snare the grains as they were blown about by the wind. Through the fleeting millennia, dunes moved and inlets opened or closed, contorting the shape of the slender ribbon of sand.

As the Banks continued their westward movement during the past 15,000 years, they rolled over and over like a log of sand kicked along by the wind and rising seas. As dunes advanced, they covered existing trees in their path while uncovering the stumps of former forests in their trail. Scientists estimate that the shoreline retreated westward nearly a thousand feet for every one-foot rise in sea level, indicating that the Outer Banks could have been more than thirty miles farther to the east at one time. It is likely that they will continue to move to the west, and the rapidity with which the barrier islands change is portentous for those who dwell there and for the structures they build upon the shifting sand.

Indian Settlement on the Outer Banks

Before the ice caps began to melt, the ocean level was lower, and land areas now underwater were exposed. The islands of Alaska's Aleutian chain are the fragmented remnants of a land bridge that once connected the continents of Asia and North America. Hunting and gathering tribes from Asia followed woolly mammoths and other animals as they migrated across the connecting path between Siberia and Alaska and were isolated in the New World when sea level rose again. These nomads roamed southward and eventually populated the continent, giving themselves names like Sioux, Cherokee, and Algonquin. When they were met by Europeans who arrived on the eastern coast several thousand years later, they were believed by the newcomers to be inhabitants of India and were mistakenly called Indians.

The Algonquin tribe probably arrived at the Outer Banks of North Carolina around 500 A.D., and they were still there to greet the first Europeans. Their friendliness to the English and Spanish was to cost them dearly, for their lack of resistance to diseases brought by the white colonists led to decimation of the tribe by tuberculosis and smallpox. By 1750 the Algonquins of

Cape Hatteras had disappeared, but many lyrical Indian words are still found on the Banks in place-names like Hatteras, Kinnakeet, Roanoke, and Kitty Hawk.

European Arrival

Both Spain and Portugal took the early initiative in exploring the New World, with England close behind as King Henry VII sent John Cabot on one voyage of discovery in 1497 and then another, in 1498, from which the explorer failed to return.

France was the last of the four major maritime powers of Europe to take an interest in western exploration. Early in the sixteenth century, that country funded a voyage by Giovanni da Verrazzano, an Italian navigator. His exploratory mission in 1523–24 led him up the eastern coast of North America. As he sailed along the Outer Banks of North Carolina, Verrazzano was profoundly deceived by what he saw. Because the barrier islands are so far from the mainland, and because he was forced to remain at a distance to avoid shoals and stormy seas, he believed he had found an isthmus separating the Atlantic from the Pacific Ocean.

In 1584 Sir Walter Raleigh was granted territory to establish a colony on the eastern coast of North America. His ships left the familiar Gulf Stream to approach Verrazzano's "isthmus," but they found no Pacific Ocean on the other side. Instead, his captains crossed a small inlet through the narrow strip of islands and chose a spot as the site for the first English colony on the continent.

His efforts were ill fated, for the first colonists became discouraged by their Spartan existence at the small fort and soon returned to England. In 1587 a new group of one hundred men and women returned to the site, which they now called the "Cittie of Raleigh." There John White's daughter gave birth to Virginia Dare, the first child born to English parents in America.

This colony also failed to prosper, and Virginia Dare, along with the rest of the colonists, mysteriously vanished. Some believe the residents of this "Lost Colony" abandoned their settlement to live with the Indians on Hatteras Island.

It was more than a hundred years after the failure of the "Cittie of Raleigh" that Bath, the first town in North Carolina, was founded. The location of Bath on Pamlico Sound encouraged the settlement of Hatteras Island by pilots and boatbuilders who catered to the fleet of small craft needed to run the gauntlet of inlets and shoals around Hatteras and Ocracoke islands.

Life on Hatteras Island during the Colonial Period

By the late seventeenth century, farmers and herders began to use the islands as pasture for their livestock. In taking advantage of the natural confinement of the ocean and sound waters, however, they allowed their cattle, hogs, and sheep to destroy much of the islands' natural cover, causing the sand to blow more easily and affecting the formation of protective dunes.

From 1690 until 1718, pirates roamed freely off the coast of North Carolina. Some of the world's most notorious buccaneers used the Outer Banks as their home bases, including the infamous Edward Drummond, also known as Edward Teach or Blackbeard. An inlet near the town of Ocracoke is known as Teach's Hole, and tales of his hidden treasure still stir interest.

Many unsavory characters inhabited the islands during this period when piracy flourished along the eastern shores of the state. Their presence and the self-reliant, independent attitudes of Outer Banks residents caused all the isolated islanders to be viewed with distrust and suspicion by mainland dwellers. Stories circulated claiming that those who lived on the Outer Banks were scavengers who used trickery to cause ships to wreck on the Banks. Most islanders regarded salvage as an honest occupation, and the wrecks added extra supplies and an element of excitement to their frugal existence, but it is uncertain whether they lured any of the dozens of ships that wrecked there each year.

The weather and ocean conditions at Hatteras by themselves were more than enough to destroy any sailing craft. The waves that pound the shoreline at Cape Hatteras, unlike those at most beaches, do not curl gracefully against the beach and roll gently back to sea. Their powerful force is vented as far offshore as the eye can see, and then again as they viciously strike the beach. The ocean explodes into spectacular geysers of white foam from the waves that smash against each other and against the shoals that fan out from the cape. Tatters of foam skitter across the beach like white tumbleweeds, snatched away by the wind from the long, sudsy arcs that form at the highest reach of the tide. Shore birds trot eagerly up and down the beach, plunging their long beaks into the sand to extract unfortunate coquinas and sand fleas left exposed by the ebb of the powerful, scouring waves. The same forces that create havoc for burrowing crustaceans and mollusks can also devastate shipping. The turbulence generated across Diamond Shoals is tremendous, and through the years it has ground many proud and stalwart ships into scattered bits of wood and rusty scraps of iron, shattering the lives and dreams of individuals with equal vigor.

The shoals claimed victims at a devastating rate that increased as shipping expanded during the four hundred years following European occupation of the New World. A chorus of pleas for a signal to warn of the insidious dangers of the shoals arose from sailors and ships' captains who traveled around the eastern tip of North Carolina. But because of the lack of an organized government among the colonies, there was little impetus for building lighthouses or other warning signals along the sparsely populated shores of America. England was more concerned about marking her own shores than those of the New World three thousand miles away.

Finally, in 1715, merchants and shippers united to establish the first lighthouse in America on Little Brewster Island to protect shipping in the heavily traveled entrance to Boston Harbor. It took another century and a revolution to change the lackadaisical attitude toward marking many of the other dangerous areas of the North American shoreline. But the English colonies thrived in America, and increasing numbers of vessels passed through the seas off Cape Hatteras. As more and more ships piled up on the sandbars, pressure mounted to provide a warning signal for Diamond Shoals.

3

The

First

Cape

Hatteras

Lighthouse

In 1773 the Cape Hatteras lighthouse was just the beginning of an idea for Alexander Hamilton. That summer, at age seventeen, he was aboard the ship *Thunderbolt* when she caught fire and nearly sank a few miles east of Cape Hatteras. After the tumultuous seas caused coals from the cooking fire to ignite the ship, some of the sails were burned so severely that there was fear the craft would be swept out of control onto the deadly nearby shoals. Fortunately, the captain was able to guide the disabled ship on its way, and those on board were thankful to escape the stormy seas off Hatteras. For Hamilton, a young man on his first ocean voyage, it was a traumatic experience. It is said that he was the first person to refer to that deadly portion of ocean as the Graveyard of the Atlantic.

Alexander Hamilton was born in the West Indies in about 1755. The son of James Hamilton and his common-law wife, Rachel Lavien (née Fawcett), he spent his early life on the island of St. Croix, where those who knew him claimed he was an extraordinarily brilliant child. When Alexander was only ten, his father left for St. Kitts, and his mother died soon afterward, leaving young Hamilton to fend for himself. His precocious talents as a businessman and as a writer brought him to the attention of a local minister who, along with Hamilton's employer, decided to send the boy to Boston for a university education. It was on this voyage that Alexander made his fateful passage by Cape Hatteras on his way to the colonies, where he arrived just at the onset of the American Revolution.

Seventeen years after his near tragedy in the waters off the North Carolina coast, Hamilton had risen to become the second-ranking member of George Washington's cabinet, responsible for developing the Treasury Department. He had not forgotten his experience off Cape Hatteras, and his new position gave him the power to take whatever steps he deemed necessary to reduce the hazards to sailors and passengers who traveled around the cape. Under his prodding, Congress passed an act in August 1789 that included a directive for investigating the construction of a lighthouse at Cape Hatteras, North Carolina.

This legislation, the ninth bill enacted by the First Congress of the United States, was known as the Lighthouse Bill, and it had far-reaching effects. It began the process that eventually led to the construction of several lighthouses, and in 1794, Congress authorized one for Cape Hatteras. The Lighthouse Bill also established the Revenue Cutter Service, the forerunner of the U.S. Coast Guard. It further specified that all light stations already in operation or under construction must be deeded to the United States and that their maintenance and repair would become the responsibility of the U.S. Treasury Department. Within fifty years of the bill's passage, sixty-five lighthouses had been built along the North American coast from Maine to the Gulf of Mexico.

Hamilton's next move was to assign Tenche Cox, first commissioner of revenue, the task of arranging for the purchase of a small parcel of land on Hatteras Island as the site for a lighthouse. It took eight years to complete the transaction, but four acres of windswept dunes and gnarled oaks were finally purchased from William, Mary, Jabez, and Aquilla Jennett for the sum of $50. The four owners of the land were orphans, all under twenty-one years of age, and the transaction had to be completed by their guardian, Christian Jennett. Even then, special action by the North Carolina General Assembly was required to complete the transfer, and the necessary legislation was not ratified until 1800, two years after construction of the lighthouse had begun.

Early American Lighthouses

Before the Revolution, the colonies lacked the centralized government to support an organized coastal warning system, but eleven lighthouses were built during those years: Little Brewster Island (Boston, Mass., 1715); Nantucket Harbor (Brant Point, Mass., 1746); Conimicut Island (Beavertail, R.I., 1749); New London Harbor (New London, Conn., 1760); New York Bay (Sandy Hook, N.J., 1764); Delaware Bay (Cape Henlopen, Dela., 1765); Morris Island (Charleston, S.C., 1767); Gurnet Point, Mass. (1769); Portsmouth, N.H. (1771); Thacker Island, Mass. (1773); and Nantucket Island, Mass. (1774). The relative wealth and power of the colonies are evidenced by the fact that five of these eleven lighthouses were built in Massachusetts, which did not possess the most hazardous coastline. Navigational hazards alone did not constitute sufficient grounds for placement of lighthouses. Instead, because lotteries were used to pay the initial building costs and taxes on cargoes provided maintenance funds, lighthouses tended to be erected in areas where the local population was large enough to under-write their construction and shipping was sufficient to support their upkeep. When either of those components was missing, no lighthouse was built.

North Carolina's three hundred miles of sandy shores and low-lying barrier islands represented more than one-fourth of the total coastline of the original thirteen colonies, and it may seem surprising that not one of the early lighthouses was lo-cated there. It is about the same distance between North Caroli-na's northern and southern borders as it is from North Carolina to New York, including the coastlines of Virginia, Maryland, Delaware, and New Jersey. Additionally, such known naviga-tional hazards as Wimble Shoals, Frying Pan Shoals, and Dia-mond Shoals border the coast of the state, making its waters treacherous to ships. For all its great length of coastline, how-ever, North Carolina had few deep-water ports, and thus the coastal populations—and their political influence—remained small.

The shallow inlets along North Carolina's eastern border made it impossible for deep-draft sailing vessels to approach the docks to unload their cargo except at the mouth of the Cape Fear River and at the port of Beaufort. Both of these areas were handicapped by their proximity to shifting shoals. The desig-nation "Cape Fear" more than adequately expresses mariners' wariness of the navigational hazards in the vicinity of Frying Pan Shoals. Nevertheless, North Carolina increasingly depended on the delivery of goods by sea, and by the late eighteenth century the populations around Wilmington and Beaufort had grown significantly. After the Revolution, North Carolina began efforts to mark its only two major ports to make them safe for ship-ping.

In 1784 the state selected a small island in the mouth of the Cape Fear River as the site for a lighthouse. This island, which forms the southernmost part of the state's coastline, was origi-nally called Smith Island in honor of its owner, Benjamin Smith. Covered with massive, five-hundred-year-old oaks whose misshapen branches seemed to be seeking escape from the prevailing winds, Smith Island was virtually uninhabited except by sea birds and a few pelagic turtles who struggled across the sandy beaches to lay their eggs. Creeks traversed the island, forming a mosaic of green marshes, and here and there dunes bulged upward from the cumulative effect of the wind. One dune, clearly visible to passing ships, so resembled a man's bald pate that the island later came to be called Bald Head Island.

Smith agreed to donate ten acres of his island to the state as a site for North Carolina's first lighthouse. Five years later, in 1789, the North Carolina General Assembly passed legislation to provide a lighthouse at Ocracoke Inlet, the entrance to the state's only other major port. Later that year, though, the United States took over the operation of all light stations—already constructed or under construction—and it became necessary for the general assembly to transfer both lighthouse projects to the federal government.

In 1792 Congress appropriated $4,000 to complete the Smith Island light. Progress was slow due to insufficient funding and the difficulty in transporting building materials to the site, and three more appropriations, totaling nearly $8,000, were needed before the structure was completed. North Carolina's first lighthouse was finally placed into service in 1795.

A year earlier Congress had chosen Old Rock, a twenty-five-acre island later to be called Shell Castle Island, as the location for the light in Ocracoke Harbor. Composed of the shells of countless oysters that lived there before sea level receded, the island was virtually as substantial as stone and more stable than the sandy islands nearby. Tenche Cox advertised in newspapers throughout several states for bidders to construct the lighthouse at Shell Castle Island as well as the one planned for Cape Hatteras. Two bids were received, but one of the bidders was untrustworthy and the other wanted more than $64,000—almost twice the amount appropriated—just to build the lighthouse at Hatteras. Other bids were sought, and in 1798 one was received from Major Henry Dearborn, a renowned lighthouse builder. By this time, Cox had been succeeded by William Miller as commissioner of revenue. Although Cox supported Dearborn's bid, Miller was not satisfied with the vague descriptions of how materials would be transported, and upon his recommendation the president rejected the bid. Further requests for bids were made, but Dearborn revised his proposal, and in October 1798 it was accepted at a total of $38,450. The government did not sign a contract, however, until St. Valentine's Day 1799, even though work had already begun by then.

Construction of the Shell Castle Island lighthouse was relatively simple. Workers constructed a wooden frame covered with shingles to support a lantern that gleamed fifty-five feet above the sea. The beacon was first lighted around 1800, but its career was short lived. The inlet it marked was closed by severe storms, and within twenty years of its construction there was no longer any need for a signal there. Later the tower was struck by lightning and the subsequent fire destroyed it, demonstrating the risks involved in building a lighthouse of wood.

Hazards of Sailing the North Carolina Coast

Of less immediate interest to North Carolina itself, but of immense importance to the vessels sailing its coast, was the area around Diamond Shoals at Cape Hatteras, where the U.S. Congress had now arranged for the state's third lighthouse to be placed. The government of North Carolina had done nothing to protect this dangerous shore, for there were no major ports nearby and the area was sparsely populated.

Shipping traffic around Cape Hatteras was heavy for several reasons. The tail end of the Labrador Current, sometimes called the Virginia Drift, flows southward along Carolina's eastern seaboard, and captains were eager to ride its helpful flow, for it could cut days off their travel time to the southern states or the Caribbean. A little farther offshore—a mere dozen miles in places—the Gulf Stream pushes northward at four miles per hour. This oceanic river gave sailors a welcome boost as they returned to New England or to Europe; the Spaniards sailed it so often that it became known as the Spanish Main.

But riding these streams was never a simple process, for Cape Hatteras, with its underwater extension of shoals, stabs abruptly eastward into the Atlantic, intersecting the currents and throwing them into turmoil. To avoid the projecting shoals, it was necessary for ships to skirt the coast widely to the east. In doing so, a southward-bound ship could collide with the Gulf Stream and be held in its grasp—or even forced backward. Struggling against the four-knot current, ships and their perishable cargoes could suffer serious delays. Sailing ships often tacked back and forth for days just north of Cape Hatteras, waiting for the prevailing southwest winds to subside and allow them to continue their journeys. It was not uncommon to see the white sails of a hundred ships gathered there like butterflies at a pond, waiting to round the cape.

The entire coast of North Carolina curves out farther eastward than the rest of the southern United States. The Southeastern Atlantic Basin stretches in a concave arc from Cape Hatteras to Jacksonville, Florida. This means that the northern Atlantic coast of Florida lies more west than south of Cape Hatteras. Cuba, Haiti, and Jamaica are almost due south from Hatteras, and one can easily see why the cape served as a control point for voyages paralleling the coast. Once Hatteras was rounded, it was clear sailing all the way to Cuba. Ships heading northward faced only empty ocean from the Caribbean Islands to North Carolina, and after they had skirted the southern tip of Florida, sailing was easy for a while. Sailors once chanted, "If Tortugas let you pass, then beware of Hatteras."

Even more difficult for mariners, the two opposing ocean currents often shift and converge off the cape, so the process of guiding ships safely through the region was delicate and fraught with danger. The confluence of these two ocean rivers creates such turbulence that the underwater sandy shoals, which reach

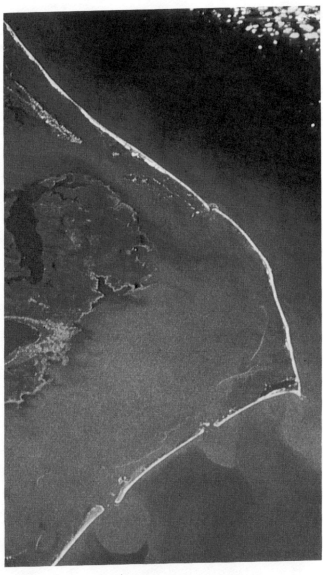

Satellite view of the Outer Banks of North Carolina.
The heavy sedimentation in the waters of the sounds and near
the inlets shows clearly, as do sandbars and shoals. The slender,
fragmented strip of land indicates the fragility of the barrier islands
and their vulnerability to the ominously rising sea levels.

like menacing talons across thirty square miles, constantly shift and reform.

Thus, although there were good reasons for ships' captains to sail near Cape Hatteras, it was with considerable trepidation that they faced the terrible shoals. Safe passage was a matter of no small concern, for the underwater dunes are sometimes 250 feet high, hiding just beneath the concealing surface of the water. Because of the tumultuous seas, the area is often shrouded in fog or mist, and the land features of the barrier islands are so low that they provide few easily visible landmarks for anxious sailors. Many times it was the thunderous crash of the breakers or the scraping of the ship's hull on underwater dunes that first told seamen they had trespassed onto the deadly shoals.

Through the centuries the shoals have waited there like a spider whose web ensnares the unwary who dare to pass too closely. The absence of ports or harbors nearby left no refuge for those unfortunate enough to be blown into the shallows by the frequent storms. Small wonder that the sea travelers who had to pass the point at Cape Hatteras demanded a warning light that would help them stay safely away from this ship cemetery. Many of those unfortunate travelers pled in vain and went down with their ships into the murky depths off the Outer Banks. When Henry Dearborn was finally hired to build a lighthouse at Cape Hatteras, it was not to guard an important commercial port, for the island was miles from any harbor; yet surely there was no stretch of coastline in greater need of a warning beacon.

Building the Lighthouse

In November 1798, Dearborn received $8,000 to purchase materials for the lighthouse. After obtaining stone in New Hampshire, he headed south toward Cape Hatteras, but his ship developed problems as it neared Boston and had to enter the port for repairs. The delay postponed the start of construction almost until September 1799. Ships carrying other supplies arrived on time, and the keeper's quarters were ready before the foundation for the lighthouse was completed.

The Cape Hatteras lighthouse was to be nothing like the flimsy tower erected at Shell Castle Island. It was designed as an imposing structure of granite, sandstone, and iron standing high above the sandy shores. To support the heavy lighthouse on the soft sand, a hole was excavated to a depth of about thirteen feet, where the sand below the low tide mark was found to be as hard and compact as concrete. On this secure footing, a solid stone foundation was laid, using mortar made by burning oyster shells at the site. The footing measured twenty-nine feet in diameter and reached to the surface, providing strong support for the massive structure that would be built above. This secure foundation was topped by a granite base nine feet thick and nine feet high, made of hammer-dressed stones ten inches thick and one to four feet long. Throughout the construction project, care was taken to see that no trees or brush were needlessly removed, for the cover helped prevent loss of sand, which was prone to drifting, in the area where the lighthouse would stand.

When winter arrived, bad weather and illness caused Dearborn to abandon the work until spring. By May 1800, work had resumed and the foundation was finished. Near the end of June, the first level, reaching twelve feet above the sand, was completed. After the crew began on the second story, Dearborn left the site to tend to other business. During that summer, sickness continued to hamper the efforts of the men left at the site. One worker died and more than a dozen others were incapacitated by serious illnesses. It was the spring of 1801 before Dearborn again turned his attention to the project at Cape Hatteras, and he continued to supervise the work until August. Long before the tower was completed, Dearborn asked for several payment advances and soon had received over $30,000 out of the total allotted amount of nearly $39,000. Sickness continued to plague the workmen, but the tower was finally completed late in 1802.

An octagonal structure, constructed primarily of brown sandstone, now reached from the foundation to a height of 90 feet. This was capped by a 10-foot-high lantern room and covered by a roof almost 5 feet high. From the base, the stone faces formed an octagonal pyramid measuring a maximum distance of 28'4" between parallel sides at the bottom, where the walls were 6 feet thick. At the top, the distance between parallel sides narrowed to 16½ feet, and the thickness of the walls was reduced to 3 feet. The stone edifice was topped by an iron-and-glass enclosure designed to hold the lantern. This circular room had a diameter of only 10 feet, a serious design flaw. A wooden stairway wound up through the interior in a spiral that stretched from the ground to the lantern chamber.

Nine years had passed since the initial decision by Congress to build a lighthouse at Cape Hatteras, and five years had elapsed from the time the cavity for the foundation was excavated until the lantern was fired in the completed structure. Construction had lagged for several reasons. The difficulty in obtaining land for the site probably was one factor that caused Congress to delay the initial appropriations for construction until 1797. George Washington was a strong advocate of a superior coastal lighting system, for he believed the U.S. merchant fleet was destined to lead the world. But by the time the go-ahead was finally given to begin construction of the Cape Hatteras lighthouse in September 1798, it was President John Adams who signed the approval of Dearborn's plans.

Bringing in the building materials was a significant engineering feat. Since the cargo ships could not reach the shore, all materials had to be transferred to flat-bottomed craft known as lighters before they could be landed. Even then movement from the shore to the site, more than a mile away across marsh or soft sand, required some ingenuity. Supplies were landed on the western side of the island, where they could be unloaded in the protected waters of the sound. Wooden tracks were laid across the dunes and swampy bogs, and oxen were used to pull carts along the primitive railway from shore to site. The mosquitoes, biting flies, and no-see-ums on the island were vicious, and many of the illnesses suffered by workers were likely brought on by insect bites or by the rugged working conditions. It has been said that it took two men to do one job—one to do the work while the other brushed away the hordes of mosquitoes.

Because Dearborn was also in charge of building the Shell Castle Island beacon, it was only after that project was completed in 1800 that he gave his full attention to the task at Cape Hatteras. He was frequently absent for long periods when distracted by other obligations. In spite of all the delays and problems, however, the first Cape Hatteras lighthouse was ready for operations by the end of 1802. The Hamilton-Dearborn tower had a focal plane nearly a hundred feet above sea level, and in clear weather the light could be seen for almost twelve miles. The building was not painted but retained its natural dark-brown sandstone color. The light consisted of a group of eighteen oil lamps with fourteen-inch reflectors. Nine cedar cisterns stored one thousand gallons of the whale oil that served as fuel for the lamps and that was provided by Stephen Hussey of Nantucket at a price of less than a dollar per cask.

Problems with Lighthouse Operations

After the lighthouse was finished, there was a brief wait of a few months before a keeper was selected and the lantern was lit. Adam Gaskins and John Mays were the two candidates who sought the duty as first guardian of the light, and Gaskins was eventually selected by the president. His salary was $333 per year, and he held the post until he was replaced by Joseph Farrow in 1808. Mays was offered the job as keeper of the Shell

Castle Island lighthouse at a salary of $250 per year, but he refused it. By the beginning of 1803, the new Cape Hatteras lighthouse was finally in operation.

For more than a year after the lighthouse was placed in service, experiments were made with porpoise oil to see if it could be used for fuel instead of the more expensive sperm whale oil, but the results were negative and the use of porpoise oil was discontinued. In 1804 the first changes were made at the Cape Hatteras lighthouse. It had been found that the lamps burned 1,400 gallons of oil annually, and the inadequate 1,000-gallon cisterns were replaced by new ones with a capacity of 2,000 gallons. In the fall of 1806, an intense storm struck the Outer Banks and damaged the Hatteras light so severely that it was out of service for over a month. Then in January 1809, the keeper spilled oil in the lantern room, causing a fire that destroyed the glass. Although Farrow obtained replacement parts from Washington, North Carolina, problems with the lantern were not solved, and sporadic fires continued to plague operations.

Before 1798 the tallest structures on Hatteras Island had been windmills, but these were dwarfed by the magnificent new lighthouse towering 112 feet above the sea and some 100 feet above the land. But beauty is surely in the eye of the beholder, for problems and complaints besieged the lighthouse from the start. Visitors and some residents declared it an eyesore because of its drab, brown color, and few sea captains were pleased with the light's performance. The temperatures produced by eighteen blazing oil lamps, all confined in a room with a radius of only five feet, were unbearable, and the keeper is said to have broken the windows several times as he recoiled from the searing heat. Geese and wild ducks occasionally flew into the glass enclosure, adding to the difficulties of maintaining the beacon. Attracted to the lantern like moths to a flame, birds would strike the windows with disastrous effect, cracking the glass and leaving the base of the tower surrounded with piles of their lifeless bodies. After a half-dozen years, a wire enclosure was woven around the top of the lighthouse, interlaced through the rails and outer braces of the lantern room, to screen the flocks of birds away from the glass.

Some observers declared the light to be visible as far out to sea as eighteen miles, but calculations show that a light one hundred feet high can be seen for less than twelve miles in clear weather. Since the weather in the region is generally anything but clear and the shoals reached eastward more than twelve miles from the shoreline, it is obvious that the Hatteras light was inadequate from the start. Also, the quality of lenses and lamps at that time was primitive. Many captains complained that even when the light could be seen, it could not be distinguished from an ordinary ship's lantern. One ship's master in the U.S. Navy declared that the Cape Hatteras light was the most important on the entire east coast, and yet he deemed it the worst light in the world. He claimed, further, that on the first nine trips he made around the cape, he never saw the Cape Hatteras light at all. Perhaps many who thought they were following a ship safely through the shoals were shocked to discover that they had been led to their doom by the lighthouse intended as their salvation. Thus, even with the new Cape Hatteras lighthouse in operation, ships continued to pile up in the Graveyard of the Atlantic and leave their remains, along with those of their crews and passengers, to be swallowed by the shifting sands of the Hatteras shore.

By 1810 the sand around the base of the building had eroded under the pressure of the steady wind, and the foundation was uncovered to a depth of four feet. It was necessary to stack brush around the bottom of the edifice to prevent further loss of sand. In 1812, after a steady barrage of criticism about its dim signals, changes were made in the lantern apparatus. Former ship's captain Winslow Lewis developed a new system of lamps and reflectors similar to a European lamp apparatus designed by Swiss inventor Ami Argand. The new-style wicks provided greater fuel efficiency, and the parabolic reflectors that Lewis attached to the lamps represented an improvement over the older equipment. Lewis had installed this system in all forty-

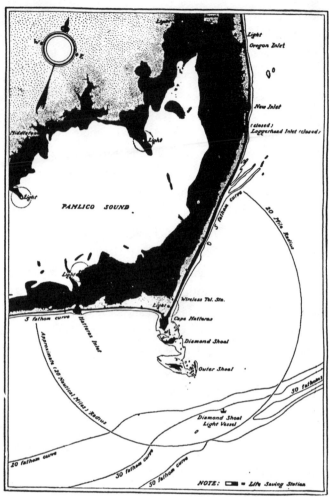

Map of the region around Diamond Shoals. The radius of visibility of the Cape Hatteras lighthouse reaches beyond the Outer Shoal, and the marker for the Diamond Shoals lightship shows how the margin of safety was extended to waters with a depth greater than thirty fathoms. (Courtesy of the North Carolina Collection, University of North Carolina Library at Chapel Hill)

nine U.S. lighthouses, including the one at Hatteras, by 1815. Although the new lighting technique upgraded the old equipment, it was still ineffective.

The range of a light is dependent upon two factors: brilliancy of the lamp and the height of the light source. The brightness of the lamp is more a function of the lenses than of the light source involved, and though Lewis's new lantern had a more efficient flame, the green glass he used for magnifying the light of the flames had a dimming effect and eventually had to be changed to clear glass.

Actions against the lighthouse by the British during the War of 1812 caused it to be closed for a brief period starting in September 1813. After the war ended, Samuel Wilkins of Ocracoke Island was hired to repair the light and rebuild the upper part of the tower, which had been damaged by British attacks.

In 1817 complaints made to the secretary of the treasury alleged that the keeper, Joseph Farrow, gave inadequate attention to his job of maintaining the light at Cape Hatteras. Captains reported that the light would often go out in the middle of the night. When inspectors came to investigate, the keeper claimed the oil was of such poor quality that it burned out every few hours. A better-quality oil was delivered, and the accusations ceased. A couple of years later, though, criticism of Farrow's maintenance of the lighthouse was renewed. The reflectors had grown so dull that the range of the light was greatly diminished, and although it was discovered that the keeper had not been supplied with the proper fluid for cleaning the reflecting surfaces, he was soon replaced. The president appointed Pharoah Farrow as the new keeper in April 1821. The inadequacies of the tower and the lantern apparatus were not remedied by the changing of the keeper, and complaints about the poor visibility of the light continued.

Interest in making the lighthouse more visible by day soon arose. The dull colors of the exterior stone facade made the tower virtually invisible against the sandy background of the dunes and through the constant salty mist that hung in the air like suspended smoke. But the miserly tendencies of government officials prevailed, and a plan to whitewash the lighthouse was abandoned. A more adequate warning signal on Hatteras Island would no doubt have reduced the number of ships that foundered in the churning shallows. In 1824, to help compensate for the inadequate performance of the lighthouse at Hatteras, a lightship was anchored at the outer edge of Diamond Shoals. Several times it drifted away from its station and had to be returned, until finally it was driven to shore and wrecked in the vicinity of Ocracoke Inlet in 1827.

The poor quality of the lamp and the inadequate performance of the keepers continued to plague the operations of the signal tower. In 1830 Pharoah Farrow was dismissed as keeper when it was discovered that he was paying others to tend the light for him while he remained at home. In 1835 the lenses of the eighteen lamps were improved with new reflectors, but within five years these also had deteriorated severely.

Some of the shipwrecks that continued to occur along the Banks attracted particular notice. Doubtless the owners, crew, and passengers directly involved in any disaster at sea consider their own tragedy to be more important than all others, but public attention has focused on only a few. One such episode was the sinking of the *Home* in October 1837. On its second sailing from New York to Charleston, the sleek new 550-ton sidewheel steamer came to public attention by making the trip in record time. Publicity for the *Home's* third excursion was high in anticipation of an even faster trip, and excited passengers crowded aboard. They would not have been so eager had they known the record that the *Home* was about to break was for loss of life in an accident at sea.

Just as the ship reached the vicinity of Cape Hatteras, a powerful hurricane called Racer's Storm swept up along a circuitous route that traversed several southern states and hit the ship head on. The violent waves quickly flooded the ship, quenching the fires of her engines and forcing the captain to turn her toward the beach. When the vessel grounded offshore, the seas ripped it apart, strewing the approximately 130 crew and passengers about in the raging surf. Only 40 survived. The death toll was the highest on record at that time for a shipwreck on the North Carolina coast.

Interest in the wreck of the *Home* was heightened by the fact that there had been only two life preservers on board; since the two who donned these preservers survived, it was believed that others might have lived had life preservers been available for all. As a direct result of this tragedy, one year later Congress passed the Steamship Act requiring that life preservers be available for all shipboard passengers.

In 1845 the original fourteen-inch reflectors in the lantern were replaced by new ones with a diameter of fifteen inches, but the improvement was scarcely noticeable. Complaints about the light continued to mount, and in 1848 a set of fifteen reflectors with twenty-one-inch diameters were installed, nearly doubling the reflecting area. Nevertheless, one navy captain still labeled it a wretched light.

In 1850, as sand continued to erode away from the foundation of the lighthouse, a fence was installed around the tower and brush was piled inside to avert additional losses. That same year, the keeper was accused of using a slave to tend the light. In 1852 a floating bell beacon was placed at the outer reaches of the shoals in another attempt to remedy some of the deficiencies of the lighthouse. This try was no more successful than the earlier efforts to place a lightship there. Within four months, the bell had vanished.

New Directions for America's Lighthouses

From 1820 until 1851, Stephen Pleasanton, the fifth auditor of the U.S. Treasury, was in charge of the development and maintenance of all lighthouses and coastal markers in the United States. Although he supervised the installation of many needed markers and beacons, Pleasanton was an auditor, not an engineer, and he was more interested in saving money than in producing architecturally and mechanically sound structures. It was his decision to continue installing the inferior lighting systems of Winslow Lewis, much to the dismay of the mariners who depended on the beacons for safety.

A typical example of Pleasanton's naïveté in dealing with the construction and operation of lighthouses was the incident of the Roanoke Marshes lighthouse. Built in 1831, this beacon had to be abandoned eight years later because rights to the land had not been obtained from the owners, who were able to obtain a court judgment to have the lighthouse keeper removed from the site. The affair was a source of embarrassment to the federal government and pointed to Pleasanton's lack of expertise in matters of lighthouse operations. Even greater evidence that something was amiss in America's lighthouse program was provided by the episode of the first Bodie Island lighthouse. Built in 1848, with Winslow Lewis again selected to install his inadequate lamp, the lighthouse soon developed a tilt, so that one side was at least a foot lower than the other. This caused concern for the building's structural integrity, as well as for the safety of the keeper, and also caused the clockwork mechanism that turned the lamp to malfunction. Pleasanton had been in charge of America's important coastal warning system since 1820, but his era of control was about to end.

In 1851 Congress demanded that Pleasanton organize a board of specialists to conduct a thorough investigation of the lighthouse establishment of the United States and to prepare a complete report. Two naval officers, two members of the Army Corps of Engineers, and the superintendent of the U.S. Coastal Survey were the chosen experts. For almost a year they made a complete study of both U.S. and European lighthouses and coastal markers. Their seven-hundred-page report was a scathing indictment of the state of America's lighthouse system and the manner in which it was funded. They confirmed what most seafarers who relied on these warning devices had been saying for years, namely that the lighthouses were not adequate to do the job. This investigation marked the beginning of a new approach to the building and maintenance of coastal warning devices in the United States. Henceforth, priority would be given to the quality of facilities and their performance. No longer would penny-pinching apply to the establishment of a proper coastal warning system. To ensure that, Congress passed a law creating a nine-member Lighthouse Board. The board was given the responsibility and authority to supervise the quality and operation of the entire American lighthouse establishment.

In 1823 the French physicist Augustin Fresnel had invented a new way of concentrating the light produced by a flame. His special system used prisms and magnifying lenses to focus the light into a powerful, directed beam. Named for their inventor, Fresnel lenses were produced in seven sizes known as orders, with the largest being designated the first order. Instead of using a multiple array of lamps and reflectors, the Fresnel system used a single lamp with rotating lenses. This new, improved lantern became available early in the nineteenth century and was used in many European lighthouses, but America continued to use the older, inferior lighting system until 1853.

As a result of the development of the improved Fresnel lighting apparatus and the creation of the Lighthouse Board, the Cape Hatteras lighthouse received a major boost to its ability to accomplish its task. In 1854 the Lighthouse Board received $15,000 from Congress to increase the height of the Cape Hatteras lighthouse to 150 feet, and at the same time the old inferior lamp arrangement was replaced by a first-order Fresnel lens system. To make the lighthouse more visible and recognizable by day, it was whitewashed for the first seventy feet from its base and the rest was painted red. The look of the dull brown sandstone that had caused some to call it ugly was now replaced by bright colors. Visibility by day and night were improved dramatically.

At the same time that these improvements were made to the lighthouse, new quarters were also constructed for the keepers. The small, cramped original dwelling was dwarfed by the new

Inside view of a Fresnel lens. The light of the small lamp inside was concentrated into a powerful beam by the intricate arrangement of the prisms. A first-order lens, the largest of seven sizes available for beacons, was first placed into the Cape Hatteras lighthouse in 1854. (Photograph by Mike Booher)

The double keepers' quarters. Built in 1854, this structure was large enough to house two keepers and their families. Today it serves as a museum and contains artifacts relating to the history of the Cape Hatteras lighthouse. (Photograph by Mike Booher)

double keepers' house, its spacious, two-story design buttressed by a long, pillared porch.

War on Hatteras Island

When the Civil War began, the strategic importance of Cape Hatteras was immediately recognized by both North and South. The government that controlled the inlets of the barrier islands clearly would dominate the sounds and rivers serving the eastern part of North Carolina. Two Confederate forts were hastily constructed at the southern tip of Hatteras Island in order to maintain control of Hatteras Inlet, the narrow portal between Hatteras and Ocracoke Islands. Also, a small group of ships was organized to harass Union vessels that ventured near the North Carolina coast. Adopting the proven tactics of Blackbeard and other pirates, this handful of Southern ships scooted in and out of the jigsaw puzzle of coves and inlets around the Outer Banks, wreaking havoc on Yankee sailing craft. Using the lighthouse as a lookout tower, observers would signal the small Southern fleet when a likely target appeared, and one of the lightly armed but maneuverable ships would slip quickly out of hiding to attack the enemy craft.

One ship alone—the *Winslow*, under Captain Thomas Crossan—captured sixteen Union vessels near Hatteras Island in just a six-week period in 1861. Pressured by the successes of this "mosquito fleet," Northern leaders in August 1861 sent seven navy ships under the command of Admiral Silas Stringham to attack the two new forts. Using long-range, rifled cannons, this naval force stood out of range of the Confederate cannons and accurately poured round after round into Fort Clark and Fort Hatteras while the Southern cannonballs plopped harmlessly into the sea. Soldiers of the New York Volunteers under the command of General B. F. Butler were landed, and the hopelessly outgunned Confederate force soon surrendered. More federal troops soon landed, and once they had control of the Banks, they used their strategic advantage to attack Southern forces along the eastern coast of the state. On the Banks themselves, life returned to a semblance of normality, and some of the local residents of Hatteras Island were able to acquire extra income by working for the Union. Many of the Northern soldiers camped around the base of the lighthouse.

When they were driven from the Cape Hatteras area, Confederate forces removed the lens from the lighthouse and, it is said, carried the apparatus up the Pamlico River to Washington, North Carolina, and eventually to Tarboro. There is no official record of the final disposition of the apparatus, but there is no doubt that the lens was removed and subsequently disappeared without a trace. The loss of the light turned out to be far more damaging to Union seagoing forces than to the Confederacy. Whereas the South had few ships traversing the area, nearly forty of the Union navy's vessels were lost on the shoals. The Union lost more vessels to the shoals than in battle with Southern forces, and some have suggested that a few more shoals might have helped the South win the war.

Colonel Rush Hawkins was placed in command of the federal forces on Hatteras. The nearest threat was from Confederates stationed on nearby Roanoke Island, and Hawkins became suspicious of their intent. He sent six hundred troops of the Twentieth Indiana Regiment under Colonel W. L. Brown to the northern end of Hatteras Island to thwart any attacks by the Southern forces. The federal troops were to establish a base camp at a small town called Chicamacomico, where they would be resupplied by an armed tug scheduled to leave Hatteras on 1 October 1861. The tug, *Fanny*, was suddenly surrounded and captured by ships of the Southern "mosquito fleet" within sight of the soldiers at Chicamacomico. The poorly supplied Southern forces were exuberant at the windfall of goods recovered from the captured tug, but prisoners taken on board spread rumors that as many as two thousand Northern soldiers were waiting at Chicamacomico to attack Roanoke. This caused dismay among the Confederate officers.

On Roanoke Island, Colonel A. R. Wright, who had not been planning to attack the Union soldiers on Hatteras, now believed that the movement of the Twentieth Indiana meant an attack on the Roanoke fortifications was imminent. He prepared a plan to trap the Northern forces by landing the men of the Third Georgia north of Chicamacomico, buttressed by North Carolina troops to be landed south of the federal encampment. Convinced that his forces would annihilate the Twentieth Indiana soldiers in a pincer movement, Wright planned to have the Confederate forces continue southward after the battle and blow up the lighthouse at Cape Hatteras.

When Colonel Hawkins saw that barges and other craft loaded with Southern troops were headed for the shore south of his camp and that the Third Georgia was approaching from the north, he realized they meant to surround his men. He quickly gave the order to retreat, and the men of the Twentieth Indiana headed southward in great haste. Many of the local residents headed out of town also, and the somewhat bedraggled group streamed to the south as rapidly as they could move through

Union troops of the Twentieth Indiana Regiment bivouacked around the Cape Hatteras lighthouse. After their twenty-five-mile march from Chicamacomico on Friday, 4 October 1861, the exhausted soldiers camped around the base of the tower. Had the Confederate forces continued their pursuit, the Union intended to use the lighthouse as a fort. (Courtesy of the North Carolina Division of Archives and History)

the hot, clinging sand. Even though it was October, the sun scorched their skin and the sand was like hot quicksand, into whose surface they sank up to their ankles.

Few of the fleeing Union troops carried sufficient water for the twenty miles of sweltering temperatures that lay ahead, and the pursuing Confederate soldiers laughed as they saw the discarded coats, shirts, and other clothing cast off by the escaping Northerners. Not until almost nightfall did the weary men of the Twentieth Indiana finally reach the lighthouse. They collapsed around the base of the tower, and some even camped inside to take advantage of the coolness there. The lighthouse was to be used as a fort if the Southern regiment attacked.

The jubilant Southerners camped a few miles north of the lighthouse to await daylight. Only then did they discover that the North Carolina soldiers had been unable to land as planned but had run aground two miles from shore. Undermanned and undergunned against the combined forces of the Twentieth Indiana and the Ninth New York regiments, the men of the Georgia Regiment were ordered to retreat to Roanoke Island. Now the tables were turned, and the next day saw the Southern soldiers in rapid retreat with federal forces in hasty pursuit. This time it was the Confederates who stripped their clothing from their tormented bodies, leaving unwanted items lying in a long gray clutter from Kinnakeet to Chicamacomico. To add to their troubles, the retreating Southern soldiers were harassed by cannon fire from Union ships just offshore.

Eventually the Confederates reached Roanoke Island, and the Union soldiers abandoned their plans for a forward base at Chicamacomico. Both sides claimed victory in the battle, but neither side suffered much damage aside from embarrassment. The debacle was quickly labeled the "Chicamacomico Races," a title aptly describing the Northern force's race to leave Chicamacomico and the Southern force's race to return to it. But the Confederate plan to blow up the Cape Hatteras lighthouse was foiled, and the United States was quickly able to replace the missing lens and restore the lighthouse to operation. Until that was done, however, ships continued to be lost in the vicinity of Hatteras.

The Lighthouse Board noted the loss of illumination at Hatteras in its 1862 report, and district engineer W. J. Newman placed a second-order Fresnel lens on the old lantern. The worn parts of the lamp were restored so that it was back in operation by the summer of 1862, but it was another year before a new first-order Fresnel lens, with all the latest improvements, was installed by federal authorities. Only then was the Cape Hatteras lighthouse functioning again at its maximum capacity.

Records of the ships lost during the war are sketchy, but one of the most famous ships to find her way to the bottom of the sea near Cape Hatteras was the first ironclad ship of the U.S. Navy, the *Monitor*. She had recently fought the Confederates' ironclad, *Virginia*, in a battle in which neither gunboat was able to secure an advantage, but the metal armor so effective in fending off cannon fire could not defend the "cheesebox on a raft" from the stormy seas around Hatteras.

In December 1862, the USS *Rhode Island* was towing the *Monitor* south by Cape Hatteras when the weather took a typical Hatteras turn for the worse. The metal-coated *Monitor* began to take on water, and before the crew could do more than cut the lines to avoid smashing against the tow craft, the armored gunboat began to founder. Forty-one of the crew were rescued, but sixteen drowned as the ship's metal plates joined the wooden timbers of the many other ships on the floor of the Atlantic at Diamond Shoals. Although lost almost within sight of the lighthouse, the sunken ship was not found again until 1973, when a Duke University research vessel located it upside down in 230 feet of water twenty miles off the cape. It is doubtful that the *Monitor* could have been saved even if the lighthouse had been operating at full efficiency, but the lack of an adequate warning signal certainly posed a threat to others who sailed near the cape until the light was fully restored in 1863.

Almost a decade would pass before any additional changes were made to the lighthouse. By then the island belonged to the residents once more, the federal troops were gone, and only the bitter memories of occupation remained.

4

The
Second
Cape
Hatteras
Lighthouse

After the Civil War, sea traffic around Cape Hatteras increased, and again the shoals began to claim their victims. In January 1867, the brigantine *George Maltby* foundered and broke up on Diamond Shoals. Within three months, the schooner *Vesta* was also lost. The owners of these vessels were outraged at the U.S. government for failing to provide an adequate lighthouse to warn of the danger.

The need to replace the old Cape Hatteras lighthouse became even more apparent when several substantial cracks formed in the aging sandstone tower; furthermore, sand had continued to erode from around the base, exposing the foundation and al-

Sketch of the first Cape Hatteras lighthouse in 1870. The change in the slope of the sides near the top shows where fifty feet of height were added in 1854, changing the focal plane of the light from 90 to 140 feet. The color scheme of white bottom and red top is also apparent from the variation in shading. (Courtesy of the U.S. National Park Service)

lowing the tower to vibrate in the wind. The keeper was hesitant to climb the rickety stairs, especially when lugging heavy cans of fuel, and when the members of Congress discovered that merely replacing the shaky, wooden steps with a new iron stairway would cost $20,000, they grudgingly authorized funds of $75,000 to begin construction of a new, first-class lighthouse at Cape Hatteras. The date was 2 March 1867.

Plans called for the erection of a new tower 600 feet north of the old lighthouse on a forty-acre tract that had been purchased from Pharoah Farrow in 1828 for $200. This new location, at least 1,600 feet from the high tide mark, would place the lighthouse safely back from the turbulent sea, in a spot sheltered from the steady winds that had continually eroded the sand from the foundation of the original lighthouse. The new structure was modeled after the successful Cape Lookout lighthouse, which had been built forty miles farther south on the remote Core Banks in 1859. It was the first of a group of four lighthouses planned to stand at forty-mile intervals along the Outer Banks, placed so that ships would never be out of sight of a beacon along the North Carolina coast. The Cape Lookout lighthouse reached 150 feet above the sand, and the smooth, red-brick cylinder was admired and emulated for its effective, simple design. Because the Hatteras light needed to be visible beyond the distant reach of Diamond Shoals, it had to be even taller than its sister beacon.

Rather than turn the Cape Hatteras project over to a private contractor, the Lighthouse Board elected to use its own engineers and to hire its own workers. Dexter Stetson, who had supervised construction of the Cape Lookout lighthouse, was hired as foreman of the project, and he and his men were on the site ready to start work by November 1868. Unfortunately, the contractors who were to deliver the construction materials had not made adequate arrangements for transportation, and the supplies did not arrive until December. After a month of inactivity, the working party was able to get the project underway, and they quickly built a tram railway one-and-a-half miles long to carry supplies to the site. As they had been for the earlier lighthouse, building materials had to be transported from ship to shore on shallow draft scows and then carted across clinging sand and watery marshes to the construction site. A substantial wooden wharf was built to provide a place where the materials could be removed from the lighters and reloaded onto the tram. Stetson first rented quarters for the workers, then, after the railway, lighters, and wharf were finished, the workmen constructed their own shelters. It was also necessary to build a blacksmith shop and storehouses, as well as derricks for hoisting the heavy stone blocks. By 1869 all of these projects were complete.

Nearly a hundred of the workers were local islanders who had been given the rare opportunity to make up to $1.50 per day, high wages indeed for most of them. Working a hundred feet or more above the ground while strong winds constantly tried to pry them from their shaky perches and a blistering sun scorched them from above made the laborers' task less than pleasant. When the winds ceased their pestering, the insects took over. They descended upon the workers in biting and irritating hordes, covering exposed skin and crawling into the eyes. But the inhabitants of Hatteras Island were used to insects, wind, and sun; they also were used to danger and hardship, for eking out a living on the remote Outer Banks usually meant fishing in the turbulent seas around Diamond Shoals, and the monetary reward for such hazardous work was much less than a dollar a day. Outsiders who visited Hatteras Island sometimes commented that the residents never had any money—or any use for it. They were self-sufficient, and when there were needs they could not meet, they bartered. Danger and hard work were nothing new for an islander.

Scows delivered the necessary 1,250,000 dark-red bricks from nearby Virginia, where they had been baked in kilns along the James River near Richmond. Nicholas Smith of Baltimore contracted for the brick at a price of $12.00 per thousand, and they were landed on the sound side of the island, where the tossing surf was not a threat. Despite this precaution, one transport sank anyway and dumped its 100,000 bricks onto the ocean floor. Metal for the ironwork and for the oil storage tanks was obtained from Bartlett, Robbins, and Company. Transportation of the supplies was contracted to Lennox and Burgess of Philadelphia, who were frequently late with the deliveries.

Stone for the foundation and steps was provided by Beattie, Dawson, and Company; in transporting it to the island, one vessel sank with its cargo of granite—yet another reminder that the sea was a constant threat.

An excavation for the foundation was made into the sand, and then Stetson found that he could not force a one-and-a-quarter-inch iron rod more than nine feet into the firm sand that began eight feet below the surface. Although pile drivers were available, Stetson decided to lay a grid of thick timbers on the compacted sand as a base to hold the heavy lighthouse. The yellow-pine beams, six inches by twelve inches in cross section, were laid in two layers to undergird the massive structure, and the foundation was further reinforced with rubble masonry and granite blocks. A two-hundred-foot tower built on an exposed beach needed considerable stability to bear the brunt of the hurricane-force winds it would frequently face.

Atop the foundation was an octagonal base of brick and granite that measured twenty-four feet high and forty-five-and-one-half feet in diameter at the lower plinth course. Upon this pedestal, the smooth, round body of the lighthouse would stand. Later, when the lighthouse was painted, the base was left in its original form with red-brick walls bordered by white stone corners. The granite used in the steps, foundation, and trim was quarried in Vermont, just across the Connecticut River from the New Hampshire quarry where stone for the original lighthouse had been obtained. White polished granite and painted bricks afforded far greater strength than the sandstone employed in the earlier structure, and its appearance was more appealing than the dull brown facade of the earlier lighthouse.

Sickness plagued the workers, as it had those who constructed the first lighthouse. Several workers had to leave the island in late summer because of persistent fevers. Stetson believed the culprit was a pond near the site, for it had become stagnant from garbage that was tossed into it daily. The pond was also a breeding ground for the many mosquitoes that in-

Base of the present Cape Hatteras lighthouse. The base was not painted, so the granite-and-brick construction looks much as it did more than one hundred years ago. Although the tower itself is circular, the base is octagonal like the original lighthouse. (Photograph by Mike Booher)

fested the site, and Stetson requested permission to drain the foul water and fill in the depression where it had been, but the request was denied.

Problems with delayed delivery of supplies continued, and once the crew was left without food for two weeks when needed provisions did not arrive on time. Only the meager rations they obtained from the islanders kept them alive. Problems with equipment, caused by sand that worked its way into all moving parts, causing wear and disruption, led to further delays. The wheels of the tram wore out continually from the friction of sand particles that penetrated the surfaces between wheel and axle.

But by November 1869, the base was finished. Next, surmounting this octagonal platform, a round, cone-shaped, brick-and-iron framework was constructed. Tapered from bottom to top, it reached upward to the lofty height where the lantern room would perch. Masons laid the circular brick walls in two layers, one inside the other with a hollow space between. The thicker outer wall was connected to the inner wall by radial brick masonry. A cross-sectional slice would have the appearance of two concentric circles connected by spokes. This feature provided the strength necessary to support the thousands of tons of the massive form. An open shaft eleven-and-one-half feet in diameter formed the interior, and a spiral metal stairway of 268 stairs led to the top. The stairway had nine flights, each ending in a landing, with succeeding landings placed on alternate sides. A window at each landing provided natural illumination.

By 1 March 1869, fifty feet of brick had been laid, and by May the tower was one hundred feet high, with four flights of the winding stairway installed. By the middle of June, the brickwork was completed to the foot of the lantern chamber and, because the metalwork for the lantern was not ready, most of the workers were sent home. In September an additional three flights of stairs were inserted when work resumed, and by October all the ironwork had been delivered to the site. At the top of the brick tower, the lantern room was placed, and above that was the lantern gallery topped by a copper roof. The lantern was completed by Bartlett and Robbins in November and was shipped within the month.

The majority of the construction was completed by the summer of 1870. From base to top, the brick tower was 196 feet high, and the iron superstructure added another 12 feet. It had taken a little more than two years to complete the structure

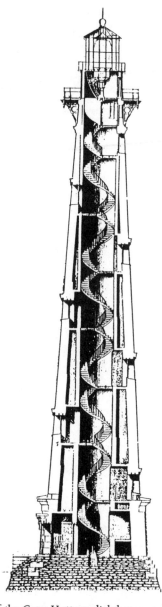

Cutaway view of the Cape Hatteras lighthouse, redrawn from the original plans, reveals the structural details of the interior, including the double-wall construction of the radial brick masonry techniques. (Courtesy of the U.S. National Park Service; redrawn by Reynold Davenport)

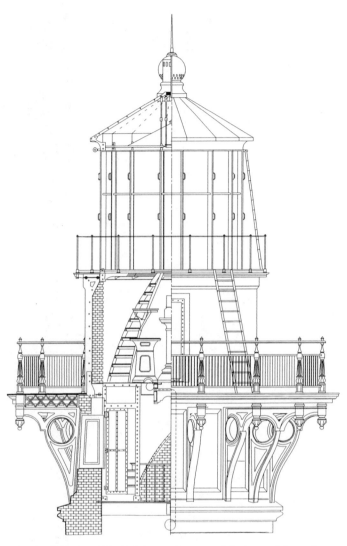

Sketch of the top of the lighthouse (not to scale). Derived from the original plans drawn in 1867, these details of the interior and exterior structure show the elaborate ironwork surrounding the balcony and the short stairway that connects the lantern to the watch room below. (Courtesy of the U.S. National Park Service; redrawn by Reynold Davenport)

Doorway to the chamber that houses the lantern. The metal enclosure with metal door helped prevent drafts that might have extinguished the lamp. (Photograph by Mike Booher)

View from the watch room to the lantern above. The last of 268 steps reach the glassed-in enclosure in which the lantern burned nightly for more than one hundred years. To fuel the lamp, the keepers once had to carry large cans of oil from the tanks far below. (Photograph by Mike Booher)

from pine-beam foundation to bright metal cap, but by mid-1870 it was ready for the final touches. The first-order Fresnel lens arrived during June 1870, and the Lighthouse Board hired George J. Crossman, an expert in the installation of lighthouse lamps, to put the apparatus in place in September. The lantern was lit in December 1870.

The total cost of building the new tower was $155,000, four times the price of the first Cape Hatteras lighthouse and more than twice the original allocation by Congress. Increasing the height of the planned 150-foot tower added significantly to the costs, and the price of the tin-lined, boilerplate oil tanks came to more than $17,000. But it had been a unique project. A brick tower more than 200 feet tall had been built on a sandy foundation in a region inaccessible by land. At 208 feet, the Cape Hatteras lighthouse was then, and still is today, the tallest in America. The lofty tower was covered with a brick-colored cement wash for protection against the weather. The lamp assembly was the best available at the time. Designed by Henry Le Paute of Paris, France, the twenty-four-sided frame of bronze contained the individually ground Fresnel lenses and prisms, which were rotated around the lamp using a clockwork arrangement powered by weights suspended in the center of the tower. As with a clockwork mechanism, the weights were cranked to the top and, as they descended to the base of the lighthouse, powered the lantern mechanism. The lenses were arranged like a giant beehive made of glistening glass and metal, and they had a jewel-like appearance even when the lamp was turned off. When the multifaceted glass prisms revolved around the glowing lamp, piercing beams stabbed the darkness in intermittent flashes whose reflections shimmered like moonlight across the waves.

Clockwork gears of the lantern. Before the lighthouse was automated, the keeper had to crank heavy weights to the top of the lighthouse, and from there they descended slowly, turning these gears and causing the Fresnel lens to rotate. (Photograph by Mike Booher)

*The base of the spiral stairway. The 268 stairs curve around
the interior of the lighthouse, intersected at intervals with landings
where windows were placed to admit light. An oil tank is recessed
in the wall behind the stairs; the well in the foreground permitted
the clockwork weights to descend into the floor for maintenance of
the mechanism. (Photograph by Mike Booher)*

Keepers of the Light

The first principal keeper selected to supervise operation of the new lighthouse was Benjamin C. Jennett, who was appointed on 30 September 1868, two years before the new tower was completed. His annual salary was $820. Jennett was assisted by C. P. Farrow and Nana S. Williams, who were each paid $400 per year.

In the early years, the heavy weights that turned the lens had to be tediously hand-cranked to the top of the tower. The rotation speed was controlled by governors, which spun the lens quickly to produce the effect of a 1.4-second flash alternating with a 4.6-second eclipse, the total cycle lasting for 6 seconds. The light source itself remained stationary; contrary to appearance and to common belief, it was not turned on and off to produce a flash. Because lighthouses are identified by their painted markings during the day and by the timing of their flashes at night, precise calibration of the rotation to produce the correct signal is essential.

The new lighthouse allowed ample working space between the hot lamp and the heavy plate-glass enclosure, eliminating one of the problems endured by the keepers of the first lighthouse. Geese continued to crash into the glass from time to time, but they caused little damage to the new, thicker glass. A set of curtains placed around the lens frame and another set inside the plate-glass enclosure protected the lamp unit from the dangers of concentrated sunlight entering through the lenses.

The first light source was a mantle lamp that burned kerosene stored in tanks built into the base of the tower. The keeper hauled kerosene up the 268 steps in five-gallon cans every day to feed the thirsty flames of the lamp, and the nine landings so thoughtfully placed at intervals along the stairway provided welcome resting places as he trudged up the spiraling stairway.

To manage all the work and the round-the-clock attention demanded by the lighthouse operation, one principal keeper

The principal keeper's quarters. When the second Cape Hatteras lighthouse was built, new living quarters for the keeper were constructed at the same time. The lighthouse required three keepers, so the principal keeper and his family lived in this dwelling, and the two assistants and their families lived in the older, double keepers' quarters. (Photograph by Mike Booher)

and two assistants were hired. A new keeper's quarters was built with stone and brick left over from the construction of the lighthouse, and the principal keeper lived in the new house while the two assistants resided in the antebellum double keepers' quarters. Water from the natural cistern of fresh water was dipped up from a well by means of a bucket suspended on a chain that rattled around a screeching pulley as it was lowered and raised. The keepers and their families raised chickens and a few pigs that were allowed to roam free in the yard and to scratch or root as they pleased. A fence kept the animals away from the small garden plots where vegetables were grown to supplement the government provisions. Many times, when bad weather prevented supply boats from reaching the island, it was the food raised by the keepers that provided their only sustenance.

Guarding the light could have been a lonely job, but there were so many chores that little time was left for loneliness. The situation was also dangerous, for there was little hope of any kind of emergency medical care should an accident or illness befall the keepers or their families. Home remedies were applied to every malady. Tins of salve and bottles of liniment lined the medicine cabinet, in which the pungent smell of camphor wafted around the vials of iodine and boxes of salts.

Sand was everywhere; it clung to shoes, stuck to perspiring skin, and was carried by the wind to infiltrate every crevice around doors and windows. On breezy days, the sand crackled like static electricity as it sprayed against windowpanes and stung the skin like sleet as it tried to penetrate every facial orifice. Clothes that were hung on the line to dry often ended up grittier than before they had been scrubbed on corrugated washboards.

Mosquitoes reigned over the swamps during the warm seasons, and when the onshore breezes died, they swarmed in great whining clouds across the beach in search of the animal blood needed to complete their life cycles. Even the wild ponies waded into the waters of the sound to escape the persistent insect attacks. A person wandering outside was likely to have any bare skin covered immediately with a dark blanket of the miniature vampires. Another voracious feeder was the green-head fly whose bite was like the stab of a hot needle.

The weather was another constant foe. Although the proximity of the Gulf Stream protected the site from extremes of cold, the constant wind during winter lowered sensible temperatures and caused one to shiver through the thickest coat. Storms struck frequently and with great severity, rattling windows, flooding the paths, and drenching the keeper as he struggled against the wind to reach the lighthouse. The powerful summer sun bleached wood to a gray patina, giving any un-

The lantern chamber. This recent photograph shows the airport-type beacon inside. The upper balcony permitted the keeper to clean the salt spray from the exterior of the glass surrounding the lantern. (Photograph by Mike Booher)

painted surfaces a silvery sheen and warping boards into twisted arcs. Uncovered skin was quickly burned to a deep copper color, and unprotected eyes developed a permanent squint as a shield against the brilliant rays of the sun that stabbed incessantly from above and reflected off the sand.

This struggle with nature extended to the care of the lighthouse itself. Brass fittings designed to thwart rust needed constant polishing to remove the green smudges of oxidation that grew like fungus on their golden surfaces. Even two hundred feet above the sea, salt spray and condensation threatened to cloud the glass in the cupola, and the windows had to be wiped daily to avoid any diminution of the lantern beams as they flashed through the Fresnel lenses like the flickering rays of a movie projector. The lenses themselves required constant care, and the wicks of the lamp needed continual trimming and examination for defects. The light had to burn unceasingly from dusk until dawn, and the keepers exercised great care to be sure it never failed. It was necessary for the principal keeper or one of his assistants to climb the tower at least twice each night to check on the lantern, and so the night watch was divided into two shifts, one lasting from sundown until midnight and the other from midnight until dawn.

The iron work used in the walkway surrounding the lantern room had to be painted often to prevent it from pitting and rusting in the salt air, and dangling precariously from a slender scaffold that swayed in the breeze at a dizzying height of two hundred feet was just part of the routine. The entire outer surface of the lighthouse had to be repainted every seven to ten years—a task that took four months.

But if there were many hardships, there were also some rewarding aspects of guarding the lighthouse. Maintaining a beacon of such great importance for mariners must have been extremely satisfying, and their role in protecting the lives of so many who depended on the warnings emitted by the Cape Hatteras lighthouse earned the keepers great respect. For men who dreamed of a life at sea, lighthouse keeping was about as close to sailing as one could come without leaving shore. The pleasant smell of salt air was always on the breeze, and the openness of the island gave residents a weather sense that is lost to those who live surrounded by buildings and other embodiments of

View at two hundred feet. Visibility from the balcony of the tallest lighthouse in America is exceptional when the weather is favorable. Cape Hatteras Point can be seen in the distance. (Photograph by Mike Booher)

civilization. Many times the keepers claimed they could "feel" the approach of a storm long before the obvious manifestations appeared.

After sundown the absence of interfering ground lights allowed the myriad stars to gleam with unusual brightness, and they freckled the night sky in glittering millions that seemed to hover barely above the top of the lighthouse. When the focused rays of the lighthouse did not intrude, and when there was no moonlight, the white swathe of the Milky Way was visible stretched from horizon to horizon.

In the late evenings, katydids and frogs that inhabited the nearby marshes in vast numbers joined their voices in a sweet cacophony, flooding the night air with their romantic serenades. The plaintive calls of chuck-will's-widows echoed across the dunes with such sad, lonely tones that one could almost believe they were the cries of lost souls. Nights were restful, with all interfering sounds and thoughts being drowned out by the regular pounding of the surf. Even storms could seem peaceful, in contradiction to their power and danger, as the rain drummed rhythmically on the roof and the wind whistled down the chimney.

The pleasures of living at the remote site must have outweighed the perils of the work and the tedium of the constant maintenance chores, because there was never a shortage of keepers for the light that guarded the Cape Hatteras shores. Lighthouse keepers were an unusual and independent lot who accepted the dangerous, demanding work willingly in spite of the small monetary compensation.

5

Winds

of

Change

When the new Cape Hatteras lighthouse displayed its light for the first time, the bright flash was visible far beyond the outermost shoal, and it was a welcome sight to seafarers. At last there was an adequate warning signal to guide them around the fearful shoals. The remains of the old tower were blown up in February 1871; the cracked and crumbling structure was in danger of collapsing and had become more of a hazard than a hazard-marker. Three mighty blasts smashed the tired old beacon and strewed fragments of its sandstone blocks in disarray across the sandy dunes. For a long time, the shattered stones of the old framework lay scattered about the site, but over time

Foundation of the first Cape Hatteras lighthouse. The sandstone base of the Hamilton-Dearborn tower is in the foreground, six hundred feet from the present lighthouse. It is all that remained when the old structure was dynamited in 1871, and even this rubble was finally washed away by the encroaching ocean in 1980. (Courtesy of the North Carolina Division of Archives and History)

they were appropriated by the island's residents for use in chimneys and the walls of houses, and eventually all traces of the original tower, except for the stump of its foundation, vanished from the area.

Although the presence of a lighthouse tall enough to beam its warning beyond the mists generated by the confluence of the Labrador Current and the Gulf Stream was a welcome relief to anyone who sailed along North Carolina's shores, no beacon had the power to alter weather patterns in the stormy Atlantic. Ships could still be caught in sudden storms or by hurricanes that spun northward out of their breeding grounds near the equator. Cyclonic winds and storm tides continued to hurl many hapless vessels into the shoals.

By the time the new lighthouse was finished, more than fifty loaded schooners were skirting Cape Hatteras every day. Several wrecked while construction was in progress and went down almost within sight of the workers, but not all of these were lost for lack of a suitable warning beacon. The winter storms of 1870 were more severe than usual, and many of the unfortunate craft were victims of the howling, relentless winds.

Bitter protests from those who lost ships and cargoes finally spurred Congress to fund new measures to reduce the losses from shipwreck. To supplement the powerful new Cape Hatteras lighthouse, additional lighthouses were scheduled to be built along North Carolina's coastline. Also authorized were seven lifesaving stations at Currituck Beach, Caffey's Inlet, Kitty Hawk, Nag's Head, Bodie Island, Chicamacomico, and Little Kinnakeet. The loosely organized lifesaving operations that had been established in 1848 by the Revenue Cutter Service were taken under the wing of the U.S. Treasury Department. For the first time, selection of crew members was based on the essential skills of boating and swimming as well as on knowledge of the sea, rather than on the old practice of nepotism. Unsupervised routines were replaced by strict rules of operation and the maintenance of a high level of discipline. The stations only operated eight months of the year, but by the early 1870s, with the new lighthouse in operation and the Life-Saving Service reorganized, sailors who ventured near Cape Hatteras could feel greatly encouraged.

The value of a well-trained lifesaving service can be seen in the contrasting examples of the loss of the steamer *Huron* and the wreck of the barkentine *Ephraim Williams*. In November 1877, the U.S. man-of-war *Huron* steered too close to the Banks while skirting the shoreline near Nag's Head in a dense fog and grounded irretrievably in the shallows. The only lifesaving station in the vicinity had closed for the winter, and no one on shore heard the frantic cries for help from the sailors stranded on the foundering vessel. The cold wind and monstrous seas snatched the helpless crewmen from the stricken craft. Washed off the slanting decks into the churning seas, only a few of the men were able to float to shore, although it was barely shouting distance away. Of the 131 officers and crew who manned the *Huron*, 103 died, making it one of the worst disasters of all time for loss of life in the Graveyard of the Atlantic.

Seven years later, on a cold December day in 1884, crewmen of the U.S. Life-Saving Service from the stations at Cape Hatteras and Creeds Hill stood on the beach watching the most vicious seas they could ever remember, whipped up by a gale that vented its rage upon the Banks. Even for a region of the Atlantic known for its turbulence, the giant breakers that formed more than a half-mile from the shore to smash on the distant sandbars were so huge they held the observers in awe. To the watchers' horror, they saw a disabled ship riding in the very midst of the terrible breakers. The ship rolled and careened about so uncontrollably from the gale-force winds and roiling seas that the men on shore believed no one on board could be alive.

The ship quickly sank into the waves until the decks were awash and only the masts continued to be visible. Suddenly a distress flag was seen fluttering from the mast, and the watchers on shore realized that someone on the ship was still alive. The crew hurriedly launched its dory into the raging surf, strapping themselves in lest they be thrown out by the surging waves. Leaning into their oars, they struggled valiantly to reach the stricken ship. As the crew of seven fought its way bravely through waves that seemed impassable, the 2,000-pound boat was tossed about like a cork and dropped into troughs so deep that those who waited on shore thought the boat had sunk.

Ignoring the grave risks to their own lives, the men in the dory reached the ship, which turned out to be the barkentine *Ephraim Williams*, and rescued the crew. When they finally struggled back to shore, the surfmen were so exhausted they had to be pulled from the boat, but they had saved every man.

There can be little doubt that without the efforts of the Life-Saving Service there would have been no survivors from the *Ephraim Williams*. Gold lifesaving medals, the highest award available in the United States for lifesaving, were awarded to

Patrick Ethridge, keeper of the Creeds Hill Life-Saving Station, and to Benjamin Dailey and five of his crewmen from the Cape Hatteras station for their dramatic and heroic rescue effort.

In 1873 an official painting scheme was established for the lighthouses along the barrier islands of North Carolina. The markings chosen for the new Cape Hatteras lighthouse were two black stripes alternating with two white stripes, which began at the base and made one-and-a-half revolutions about the tower as they swirled to the top. The twisting stripes gave the tower the striking appearance of a giant black-and-white peppermint stick. This color scheme made it immediately recognizable and perhaps, combined with the structure's height, led to its popular appeal. One keeper of the lighthouse, when asked by visitors how he managed to paint the wraparound stripes, took great delight in telling them he merely painted vertical stripes and then gave the tower a twist.

The nearby Cape Lookout lighthouse was marked with a black-and-white checkered design resembling a diamond pattern. Because diamonds seemed more appropriate for the lighthouse that marked Diamond Shoals, many believed that the painter had gotten the lighthouses confused. However, there was no such mix-up and no truth to the wry suggestion that the cans of striped paint and the cans of checkered paint had been exchanged by accident.

The next major event in the evolution of the Cape Hatteras beacon occurred in 1879, when lightning struck the tower. The iron in the structure had not been properly grounded in the deep sand, and the brickwork cracked from the force of the lightning bolt. It was necessary to bury a large metal plate in the sand to create a proper grounding for the building. This apparently met the need, for the lighthouse suffered no further damage from lightning. Nonetheless, anyone who was in the tower during one of the area's frequent thunderstorms must have felt somewhat nervous about being in the tallest lightning rod for miles in any direction.

A whistling buoy was positioned over the shoals in 1884, but it quickly drifted away, and continued efforts to keep it stationary ended in failure. In 1897, seventy years after the last unsuccessful attempt to place a lightship on Diamond Shoals, Congress authorized the anchoring of a new lightship on the outer shoal. This time the effort was successful because of improved anchoring technology, and except for those occasions when storms caused the Diamond Shoals lightship to slip its anchor or when it temporarily ceased operations during wartime, the light of a stationary vessel provided warnings to supplement those of the Cape Hatteras lighthouse for more than fifty years. But in spite of these improvements in guarding the cape, one hundred ships were lost to the shoals between 1871 and 1900.

On 31 August 1886, an earthquake rocked the lighthouse. The quake was centered at Charleston, South Carolina, and the first shock at 9:50 P.M. shook the eastern seaboard for ten to fifteen seconds. Three aftershocks followed at approximately ten-minute intervals, although none of these lasted as long as the first. The lighthouse trembled and swayed from the power of the quake, but although loose objects rattled around and it was difficult for the keeper to stand up in the tower, there was no apparent structural damage. It is possible that the crevices resulting from the earlier lightning strike expanded or that other hairline cracks developed, but it was impossible to determine whether this was so, and the lighthouse continued to flash its signal, undaunted by this new assault from nature.

Aside from the successful placement of a lightship on the Outer Diamond Shoal and the improvements in the Life-Saving Service, little changed on Hatteras Island during the first thirty years of the second Cape Hatteras lighthouse. Life on the island was much the same as it had been for a hundred years, but that situation changed dramatically with the advent of the twentieth century.

Cape Lookout lighthouse. Built before the Civil War, this lighthouse served as a model for the Cape Hatteras lighthouse and others along the coast because of its superior design. The diamond pattern of its paint scheme was mistakenly believed to have been meant for the Cape Hatteras lighthouse. (Courtesy of the North Carolina Division of Archives and History)

Diamond Shoals lightship. Beginning as early as 1820, several attempts were made to station a lightship on Diamond Shoals, but not until an improved anchoring system was developed were the efforts finally successful. From 1897 until 1967, with only brief lapses due to storm and war damage, a lightship was anchored on the outer edge of Diamond Shoals. (Courtesy of the U.S. National Park Service)

The Age of Technology

The end of the nineteenth century brought the demise of the isolation and local orientation of the Outer Banks of North Carolina. The nature of the islands made them attractive to vacationers, and some inventors found the low sandy hills and beaches ideal for their experiments. Two brothers from Ohio were among the pioneers of progress whose scientific tests near Nag's Head made that part of the Banks famous. Wilbur and Orville Wright achieved powered flight, thus removing one of the restraints that kept humans earthbound, with their first short but historic flight in the shadow of Jockey's Ridge in 1903. In 1901 Reginald Aubrey Fessenden conducted the first successful transmission of radio waves without the use of wires when he broadcast a message between Cape Hatteras and Roanoke Island.

Perhaps the invention that had the most immediate impact on the Bankers' way of life was the automobile with its balloon tires. Air-filled tires could ride on top of the soft sand, and when they were used on a motorized vehicle, it became possible to maneuver at will over beaches and dunes. Once this mode of transportation became available, it was only a matter of time until bridges and roads opened most of the region to traffic from the mainland, although ferries continued to be the only means of access to Hatteras Island.

With an effective lighthouse in place, fewer ships wandered into the area of the shoals, and with the advent of the steam engine, most captains were able to avoid being blown into the dangerous waters. The few wrecks that did occur caused only minimal loss of life, primarily because of the efforts of the Life-Saving Service, which, by 1905, was operating year-round from eleven Banks stations. As new technology became available, continued improvements were made to the system that guarded the Hatteras shores.

On 1 July 1912, the lantern of the Cape Hatteras lighthouse was improved by the installation of an incandescent oil-vapor lamp that burned with an intense white flame. The new apparatus, which used pressure to generate a mist of oil that fueled an incandescent mantle, was like a king-sized version of the pressure lanterns whose bright glow and steady hiss can be found in every modern campground. The result of this change was an increase in the intensity of the light from 27,000 to 80,000 candlepower. The device was so effective in producing a dependable, brilliant signal that no further modifications were made in the lantern for more than twenty years.

Although wrecks were rare by this time, an occasional ship still wound up stranded on the shoals. One of the most unusual ships to meet its end on the Outer Banks wrecked there in September 1913, soon after the improvements were made to the lantern. The *George W. Wells* was the first six-masted schooner ever built and, at 2,970 tons, was the largest sailing ship ever to be trapped and demolished on the biting edge of North Caro-

The George W. Wells. *The largest sailing ship to be lost on North Carolina's Outer Banks, the six-masted schooner grounded on Ocracoke Island in 1913. (Courtesy of the U.S. National Park Service)*

lina. As this juggernaut of the seas sailed from Boston to Florida, all twenty-eight sails were stripped away by a hurricane as she passed Cape Hatteras. The helpless hulk was pushed by the waves into the shallows and grounded. The giant craft was destroyed, but all her crew and passengers were saved through the efforts of the Life-Saving Service.

World War I came late to America and to the Outer Banks. The United States did not declare war on Germany until 1917, three years after the start of the war in Europe, but within six months German submarines were on their way to disrupt shipping along the eastern coast of North America. Only a few U-boats prowled off the Outer Banks, but America's unpreparedness for their vicious attacks made the work of the German commanders easy, and the results were tragic for coastal shipping. The underwater craft were able to attack without fear of reprisal, and several ships were sunk within view of the Cape Hatteras lighthouse by torpedoes, mines, and fire from deck guns.

The Diamond Shoals lightship also came under attack when a submarine fired on the anchored and helpless vessel. On 6 August 1918, men on Cape Hatteras Lightship No. 71 spotted a German sub lying just outside the shoals, and the boat's malicious intent became clear when it fired on a freighter, causing it to catch fire and list heavily. The wireless operator on the lightship quickly tapped out a warning for all ships to steer clear of the sub. When the German captain realized that the lightship was warning his intended prey, he ordered the crew to abandon the vessel. He then turned his guns on the deserted craft and sank it. Before the United States was able to develop defenses against the Germans' undersea tactics, the war ended, and the solution to the problem of submarine warfare was left for another conflict.

In 1915 the Revenue Cutter Service and the Life-Saving Service united to form the U.S. Coast Guard. While the war was on, the Coast Guard operated as a branch of the Navy Department, but when hostilities ceased it returned to the domain of the Treasury Department. After the war, the principal responsibility of the Coast Guard was to protect shipping and save lives along America's shores, including North Carolina's Outer Banks.

6

The

Lighthouse

in the

Twentieth

Century

When Unaka Benjamin Jennette became keeper of the Cape Hatteras light in 1918, it seemed only natural that he should serve as its guardian, for the history of the Jennette family was intertwined with the history of the lighthouse.

After the land for a lighthouse was purchased from the four orphaned Jennett children, more than half a dozen relatives manned the Cape Hatteras lighthouse. Joseph C. Jennett was hired as keeper in 1842 and Benjamin C. Jennett in 1868. Other family members served as assistant keepers, including William in 1860, Wallace in 1863, Joseph E. in 1869, Zion in 1870, and Joseph B. in 1889. Somewhere along the way, an "e" was added to the family name, so that by the twentieth century *Jennett* had become *Jennette*. Two of Unaka's brothers served as lighthouse keepers, too—one at Cape Henry, Virginia, and the other at Rock Point, Maryland.

When Unaka Jennette moved into the principal keeper's quarters, the terrain was different from that seen today. There were no high dunes like those built later by the WPA, and the flat sand often flooded when storms raged at high tide. About the only tracks marring the vast expanses of pearly sand were hoofprints of the horses that roamed the island. Sometimes cattle also ventured out of the patches of twisted cedar and yaupon, leaving a winding, dotted trail to mark their path until it was erased by the next high tide. The grass that grew near the lighthouse was kept cropped short through continual feeding by the wandering cattle and horses. No tall trees grew nearby, and on clear days the scattered cabins of a distant fishing camp could be seen south of Cape Point.

A car track bordered by sprawling yaupon and scattered scrub oaks led to Buxton, the nearest town. Walkways surrounded the double keepers' house as well as the principal keeper's quarters, and these were connected by a brick walk that led to the lighthouse. A fence separated the two dwellings, and it always gleamed brightly from frequent whitewashing.

In addition to the shed where oil was formerly stored, there were a few other outbuildings. Each keeper was furnished a small storage shed in which livestock feed and tools were kept, and outdoor privies substituted for modern plumbing. Before electricity was available for refrigeration, a cool bin with three compartments, one for each keeper, was used for storing milk, eggs, fruit, and vegetables. Once, in the late 1920s, a banana boat ran aground at Hatteras Inlet, leaving its cargo of fruit to rot on the beach. All the local residents, including the keepers, salvaged what they could and lugged countless bunches of the luscious cargo home. As the cool bin was full, a large closet in Jennette's house was stacked to the ceiling with hundreds of pounds of green bananas. Fruit was a rarity, so the bananas were consumed with relish from the time they were half-ripe until they were exceedingly overripe. By the time the last mushy, brown remnants were discarded, they were surrounded by swirling clouds of fruit flies, and no one at the lighthouse could bear the sight of a banana.

Winter heating was provided by fireplaces and heaters, and neatly stacked woodpiles lined the yard. Some of the wood was driftwood; it was easy to find and always burned with unusual-colored flames. Each dwelling had a summer kitchen in which the keepers' families prepared their meals until an oil-burning cookstove was finally installed in the main kitchen. Although oil heaters eventually reduced the need for wood, fireplaces continued to provide crackling comfort on cold, stormy days. Illumination came from oil-burning lamps that produced flickering, ghostly shadows on the walls but were so inadequate for reading that everyone usually went to bed shortly after sundown.

The keeper and the two assistants shared equally in the task of keeping the light burning from dusk till dawn and in the constant maintenance chores that occupied the daylight hours. When major lighthouse repairs were required, working parties came from Portsmouth or Baltimore.

Painting of the lighthouse was usually contracted out, although local residents were sometimes hired to help. The keeper and his assistants did simple touch-up work suspended from a bosun's chair. When a complete paint job was required, a special paint box, as it was called, was devised, consisting of a large curved bench about twenty feet long, six feet wide, and with a four-foot-high safety rail. The box was curved so that it fit closely to the rounded surface of the lighthouse, and the painters sat on this as they applied paint to the brick tower. The apparatus was raised and lowered by a rope secured to the rear bumper of Jennette's Model A Ford. When the bench needed to be raised, someone would drive the car forward, and if the painters needed lowering, the car would chug a few feet backward through the sand.

Painting while suspended high in the air and clinging to a narrow bench supported only by a rope could be a sobering experience. This was definitively proved one day when Jennette noticed that a couple of the workers who had been hired to help apply paint were secretly partaking of some bottled spirits. As they swayed uncertainly on their high perch and smeared paint without inhibition but with great lack of purpose, Unaka drove the car forward and then did a quick reverse before coming to a sudden stop. The suspending ropes twanged threateningly as the slender seat carried the men upward rapidly, then just as quickly plunged them downward to a jolting stop. The incident did not seriously endanger the men, but it managed to get their attention and squelched any future inclinations to imbibe on the job.

Medical necessities, including pulling teeth, were usually attended to by the keeper, but there was a local pharmacist and also a midwife who helped out when more expertise was called for. The midwife was needed frequently, for Jennette and his wife had seven children, five of whom were born at the keeper's residence. It was typical of lighthouse keepers to have large families, perhaps because the many chores were made easier by the availability of additional hands. A doctor from Michigan moved to the island in the early thirties, and she quickly endeared herself to the residents.

Life at the lighthouse was never lonely for the Jennette children, and in fact there was much that made it exciting. Their father allowed them to watch passing ships through a spyglass from the top of the lighthouse, and he often climbed the numerous stairs carrying a heavy can of oil in one hand and a child in the other. When the lantern was in operation, the golden flash of the revolving Fresnel lens was a fascinating and beautiful thing for the children to watch and was also a great attraction for visitors. Twelve feet high and six feet in diameter, the Fresnel apparatus had twenty-four bull's-eye magnifying lenses equally spaced around the center to enhance the beams from the glowing mantle. The mantle was only six inches high and three

Bull's-eye of a Fresnel lens. As the massive array of prisms turned around the internal lamp, the light was concentrated into a powerful beam that flashed through this circular lens. This action produced an effect that caused many to believe that the light winked on and off. (Photograph by Mike Booher)

inches in diameter, but over a thousand individual glass prisms reflected the light from above and below, so that 85 percent of the light's energy was concentrated through the bull's-eyes.

Visitors at the lighthouse were common, especially on Sundays, and Unaka, or "Naka" as he was called, always took time from his busy schedule to give them a tour. The visitors sometimes brought along children of their own who provided ready companions for the Jennette children in games of croquet or hide-and-seek. There were five families at the nearby lifesaving station, and a strong sense of community developed among the residents.

Every day brought a trip to the mail landing, usually by horse and cart, and the youngsters were allowed to go along. Meeting the mail barge was a big event because of the interest in what the boat from Manteo might bring—not just mail, but supplies and special visitors as well. Unless one has lived in an isolated spot, it is difficult to comprehend the thrill that the arrival of goods and company provided to the residents of remote islands like Hatteras. News from the mainland and special foods that were unobtainable locally were especially welcome treats. Meeting the mail barge was almost like having Christmas every day.

There were, in fact, two Christmas celebrations on Hatteras Island. On 25 December, everyone gathered in the Methodist Church. Parents brought gifts for their children and hung the colorful surprises on a giant tree erected inside the church. Sometimes the gift-laden tree would sag clear to the floor from the weight of the presents. The church added to the good cheer by giving candy and an apple and orange to each child. On 5 January, the residents observed Old Christmas, and again each child received a small gift and some fruit.

The children had to help with the multitude of chores associated with life at a lighthouse, but there was still plenty of time for fun. The youngsters looked forward each year to the first day of May, when they were allowed to remove their shoes and frolic barefooted on the warm sand for the duration of the summer. Many of the guests who spent the night at the lighthouse were ships' captains who entertained the children with true tales of seafaring adventures. Two ponds occupied the area behind the dwellings, and these shallow pools of fresh water, each only about six feet deep, were the habitat of a variety of interesting creatures. Turtles, fish, water birds, and cottonmouth moccasins resided there among the cattails and lily pads. Unfortunately, the pools also served as convenient breeding grounds for mosquitoes.

Virtually all travel on the island was either by horseback or by horse and cart. Unaka Jennette owned one of the two motorized vehicles on the island, and his Model A Ford served as the ambulance when one was needed. There were no real roads on the island, only meandering, two-lane ruts called car tracks, and even these were scarce. There was very little need for transportation, and it was only for trips to the Buxton stores, to church, or to the mail docks that the Ford was cranked up. For longer trips, a typical practice was to drive along the hard-packed sand at the edge of the surf while the tide was out, for otherwise the clinging sand would easily cause the car to become stuck. It was impossible to take a trip of any significant distance without ending up covered with sand from head to foot from all the digging and pushing needed to keep the frail vehicle from becoming a permanent captive of the grasping soil.

Jennette owned cattle and horses and, like the other residents, he allowed them to roam at large on the island. All livestock owners marked their animals with ear cropping or other types of branding so that they could be identified. Once a year, the cattle were rounded up so that the animals could be dipped to eliminate ticks. The roundups were cooperative ventures, and the residents helped each other gather the reluctant animals and run them through a vat containing the dip. Each dipped animal was then slapped on the rump with a paintbrush covered with green paint to signify the completion of the process. Unfortunately, tick-borne disease swept the island despite these precautions and drastically reduced the numbers of healthy livestock.

Supplies that could not be produced by the keepers and their families were brought in once a month by boat, usually a buoy tender. This process of "grubbing up" was always exciting. Hardly ever did specialty items last for a whole month, and it was a great delight to have longed-for goods on the pantry shelves again. Sugar, coffee, tea, and flour were regular staples on the monthly list, as were less enduring articles like fruit or candy. The arrival of the supply boat was also an occasion for resupplying medications and spices. When it arrived, Jennette and his assistants used a local gas boat to get out to the tender, where they would usually eat dinner with the crew. Later the crew would load the ship's boats to the gunwales with supplies and run them aground in the shallows at the mail landing; from there the goods had to be transported the rest of the way by hand through waist-deep water.

Occasionally the lighthouse was visited for inspection by the lighthouse superintendent. These were scheduled visits, and before the inspector's arrival everything had to be cleaned or painted. Even the furniture was brought outside and aired. Although there was some anxiety about the scrutiny, the lighthouse was always kept in excellent condition, and the stopover tour provided a welcome change in the routine. Visitors from the mainland were also welcomed as a source of information about events unknown on the isolated island. Because there were no radios, televisions, or telephones, this was often the only way to keep up with news on Hatteras. Strangers were always recognizable by their speech, for the unique speech patterns on Hatteras Island were so distinctive that no one from the mainland could ever be confused with a resident, even if the visitor was only from as far away as the nearby North Carolina coast.

There were few public services on Hatteras. The island children attended grades one through eleven at Buxton School. (In those years there was no twelfth grade in North Carolina schools.) There was no fire department on the island, only an organized bucket brigade that used an old hand pump. There was little need for law enforcement.

The Threatening Sea

The beach in front of the lighthouse alternately shrank and expanded as storms and currents influenced the shape of the point at Cape Hatteras. The continual sweep of the Labrador Current moved sand from north to south in the fashion typical of the longshore current, depleting one area of beach while enriching another. This migration of sand from one area to another that caused the beach between lighthouse and sea to shrink is not technically erosion, but, according to scientists, is called shoreline retreat. Movement and distortion of the Banks has maintained the sandy bar in a state of equilibrium. Early maps of the region show that, although localized distortion and some westward movement have taken place, the overall shape of the barrier islands has changed little in five hundred years.

Most of the changes in the dimensions of the beach between the lighthouse and the surf were not due to erosion but rather to flooding caused by land submergence. During the nineteenth century, the beaches at Hatteras were extremely flat, and a very small increment in the gradually rising sea level could cause water to cover a significant expanse of shore. From 1802, when the first lighthouse was placed there, until 1870, when the second beacon was built, an average of fifty feet per year was lost to submergence. The natural slope of the beach steepened near the lighthouse, and even though the sea continued to encroach, the rate of flooding was gradually reduced by half, so that between 1870 and 1914 the shoreline advanced by only twenty-five feet per year. By that time, the slope of the shore had become so steep that erosion did begin to factor into the loss of beach.

In 1919, soon after Jennette assumed the keeper's job, a portentous event brought new attention to the Cape Hatteras lighthouse and raised worries about its continued function. Observers suddenly noted that the advancing surf was no more than the length of a football field away from the foot of the tower. The sea that had once seemed so distant now seemed to threaten destruction. That the sea had taken over a hundred years to cover a mile, and that the rate of submergence had slowed drastically as the slope of the beach increased, went unnoticed. Everyone's attention focused instead on the surging, looming menace of the ocean.

Concerned individuals began restoring the shrubs and grasses that had once covered the sands in abundance. They constructed dunes all along the shore in an effort to stall the advance of the sea. Soon—probably more as a result of natural fluctuations than of these artificial measures—the beaches stabilized, but the Lighthouse Service and the Coast Guard kept a nervous eye on the slender margin of safety that remained between lighthouse and tide. After 1920, once the beaches were more secure, life on the Banks returned to normal.

Because of technological advances, some the result of wartime experiences, the number of ships beaching themselves on North Carolina's outer islands decreased significantly in the early twentieth century. Jennette continued to make sure that the lantern beamed its warning flashes across the waves, but in spite of this, one highly publicized shipwreck did occur in 1921. On a cold January morning, a five-masted schooner was sighted aground on the outer shoal. She still carried full sail and, though stuck firmly in the sand, displayed no distress signals. When the lifesaving crew reached the vessel, they found freshly prepared food in the galley pots and tables laid out for a meal, but the only living thing left on board was the ship's cat. The two anchors and the lifeboats were missing, but there was no evidence of violence. The ship, the *Carroll A. Deering*, became one of the most famous mystery ships of the Outer Banks. It was a topic of discussion for weeks by those who lived at the lighthouse, but no one ever found the missing crew members or explained their strange disappearance.

Jennette saw fewer ships meet destruction on the shoals than had any keeper before him. This decrease in ship losses also reduced the need for men to serve at the lifesaving stations. A concurrent decline in the fishing industry brought financial depression to the islanders long before the stock market crash of

1929, and the isolation of the area continued to hinder expansion of commercial activities that might have produced more jobs or generated a growth in population.

The loss of traditional revenue-producing occupations caused many Outer Bankers to move away, but as 1930 approached, important changes took place that would alter forever the nature of Outer Banks existence. In 1927 Wash Baum, chairman of the Dare County Board of Commissioners, persuaded the North Carolina General Assembly to allow the sale of bonds to pay for the construction of a bridge across Roanoke Sound. Less than two years later, a group of businessmen from Elizabeth City arranged for construction of a bridge across Currituck Sound. The year 1928 saw the completion of the Roanoke Sound Bridge, which connected the Nag's Head area with Roanoke Island, and by the end of 1930 the Wright Memorial Bridge crossed Currituck Sound twenty miles farther north. Although the bridges were built with private funds, the state purchased both by 1935 and eventually constructed paved roads that reached from the Wright Memorial Bridge to the small village on the southern tip of Ocracoke Island. Ferry service joined the portions of Highway 12 divided by Oregon Inlet on the north of Hatteras Island and Ocracoke Inlet on the south. Unrestricted access to the Nag's Head area soon opened it to mushrooming development, but the limits of ferry travel stifled similar development of the southern islands.

In the 1930s, scientists understood the dynamic nature of a barrier sandbar even less than they do today, and many believed that the stability of the islands was assured by the restoration of ground cover to hold the sand. When the beaches in front of the lighthouse began to disappear once more, the response was an influx of workers from the Civilian Conservation Corps (CCC), who joined local residents to plant more grasses and trees and to place wind fences up and down the Outer Banks. Residents assumed that these efforts would cause dunes to develop along the beaches, and the dunes in turn would defend the narrow, sandy islands from the devastating effects of washover during storms. The project would also provide relief for many impoverished people desperate for work.

The CCC and its allies planted thousands of trees and low shrubs, as well as hundreds of acres of sea oats and other grasses. They strung miles of wire-and-slat wind fences along the beaches near the tide line. Stretching like rolling waves of picket fences, these windbreaks functioned like wooden nets to catch and hold the blowing sands. When dunes began to develop, a collective sigh of relief seemed to echo in the whisper of the wind that ruffled the newly planted sea oats along the shore. Few of those involved in the project understood that the barrier islands perpetuate themselves by retreating before the rising ocean, and that covering the sands with new foliage could do little more than slow the western movement.

Other schemes of similarly questionable value were put forward to save the beaches from washing away. Sand replenishment, a process in which sand was pumped from the sound or ocean floor to fill gaps in the beach, offered quick results, but the sand removed from the ocean floor left cavities that changed the behavior of ocean waves and often increased their erosive action. Dredging changed the slope of the ocean floor from a natural, gentle curve to an abrupt ridge, causing the waves to strike the shore with greater force and leading to more rapid beach loss.

Concurrent with the CCC's massive reclamation effort, other coast watchers originated a plan to prevent extensive development of Hatteras Island. Those who saw how quickly the Nag's Head area became built up hoped to maintain Hatteras Island in its natural state by having it declared a national seashore park. In 1933 local initiative began to stimulate state and national interest in a plan to make all of Hatteras Island, except for already existing villages, part of a protected region that would extend from Oregon Inlet to Cape Lookout. Later that year, two severe hurricanes struck the islands with strong winds and roaring seas that stripped away dunes and damaged hundreds of houses. Impressed by the urgent need for action, the federal

Civil Works Administration spent $1 million on additional efforts to protect the Banks from damage.

When the first hurricane hit, the keepers and their families remained at the Cape Hatteras lighthouse to ride out the storm. The keepers had to stay, for the light could not be allowed to go out. The previous summer had been extremely dry, and even the ponds behind the keepers' quarters had dried up until cracks formed a geometric mosaic in the mud at the bottom. Nevertheless, there was little room for the immense quantities of water that accompanied the furious storm. Along with the heavy downpours came a surging mass of sea water pushed along by eighty-five-mile-an-hour winds. The sidewalks leading from the quarters to the lighthouse were soon under about a foot of water. To reach the lighthouse, Jennette and the two assistants had to lock arms and slosh three abreast through the rising water to avoid being blown down by the powerful winds. Their families remained in the houses, awed by the force of the storm. When the wind and rain finally abated, the sandy ground was completely saturated with water, and large areas were still covered with large puddles that had nowhere to go. Debris was scattered everywhere, but there was relatively little damage to the dwellings, and the lighthouse itself stood as strong as ever.

Before the standing pools of water could evaporate or sink into the water-logged ground, another severe hurricane appeared on the horizon. Jennette and his assistants quickly took their families into Buxton rather than have them remain to face another tempest on the exposed tip of land where the lighthouse stood. Then the keepers returned and carried food and other supplies into the lighthouse, where they intended to ride out the coming cyclone.

These were wise precautions, for with the soil already drenched, any new rainfall would collect above ground and flood the island. Indeed, when the maelstrom hit, the torrential downpours and tidal surge caused water to enter the lighthouse. It seeped in through cracks surrounding the door and rose to swirl menacingly about the men inside. Unaka Jennette remained on the first floor as long as possible, but when the water climbed to his chin, he and his assistants had to move up the stairs. The giant tower, sturdy as it was, rocked and swayed under powerful wind gusts, but the lantern was kept burning without letup, and the keepers stuck to their job faithfully. Never did they even consider abandoning their post, despite fears of drowning or being crushed should the lighthouse collapse.

After hours that seemed like days, the 125-mile-an-hour wind finally ceased its thunderous roar and the water gradually receded, allowing the men to leave. Jennette had nailed a large dining table against the door of his residence to keep the water out, but the waves that struck the lighthouse and the dwellings at a speed of greater than 50 miles an hour and a force of 10,000 pounds per square foot were not to be thwarted, and the door was forced open. The water flooded the interior of the living quarters to a level more than waist high, ruining the furniture and everything inside. The three keepers walked grimly to Buxton, filled with trepidation as they viewed the devastation, but they found that their families had also made it safely through the worst storm they could ever remember. It was the last time that the families of the keeper and his assistants would ever live at the lighthouse.

In 1934 electricity became available for use at the lighthouse. Two Kohler generators and a large bank of batteries were placed in the building that had been used earlier to hold the oil supplies, although later they were moved to the principal keeper's dwelling and placed in an upstairs room. The oil-burning mantle lamp in the lighthouse was replaced by an electric bulb.

In 1935 four individual landowners, in an attempt to encourage the development of a seashore park, donated to the state of North Carolina a thousand acres of land surrounding the Cape Hatteras lighthouse. The North Carolina General Assembly, impressed by this gesture, passed legislation to prevent livestock from roaming free on Hatteras Island. The law supported the

Unaka B. Jennette, the last member of the Lighthouse Service to serve as a keeper of the Cape Hatteras lighthouse. Before the lighthouse was closed in 1936, polishing the elaborate lens system was one of the constant chores he performed routinely. (Courtesy of the U.S. National Park Service)

ongoing efforts to reestablish vegetation on the sandy shores. Rather than fence up the half-wild animals, residents sold most of their stock to farmers on the mainland. The National Park Service, also interested in the development of a national recreational park on the Outer Banks, joined in the reclamation efforts.

In 1936, despite all efforts to stop them, waves reached the base of the Cape Hatteras lighthouse, where they curled around the granite-and-brick foundation and threatened to undermine

Unaka B. Jennette and sons. The former keeper of the Cape Hatteras lighthouse stands between two of his sons in front of the principal keeper's quarters in 1962. On the left is Almy Jennette, and on the right is Rany Jennette, who works as a National Park Service ranger at the Hatteras Island Visitors' Center in Buxton, North Carolina. (Courtesy of Rany Jennette)

it. The long-dreaded decision at last had to be made, and the sixty-five-year-old lighthouse was abandoned. It had been in service just five years less than the original Cape Hatteras lighthouse, but unlike its predecessor, it was still in good condition when it closed.

Unaka B. Jennette supervised the last "lights out" call on 15 May 1936. He had watched over the beacon for eighteen years. The emptiness the islanders experienced at the loss of their lighthouse was overwhelming. The omnipresent flashing signal that had not missed a blink in fifty years was as much a part of life on Hatteras as the sun or moon, and its loss hardly seemed less important. Not long thereafter, the Lighthouse Service was eliminated and the Coast Guard took over lighthouse operations in the United States. The simultaneous demise of the lighthouse and the Lighthouse Service seemed to mark the end of an era.

Jennette did not believe the lighthouse should be closed, and he was saddened when it was shut down. Until 1939 he continued to serve as lighthouse keeper at a substitute tower a mile and a half away in Buxton Woods, and then he watched over the Roanoke Marsh lighthouse until he retired in 1943. The useful life of the Cape Hatteras lighthouse was not over, but none knew that then, and it was left to stand dark and deserted for nearly two decades.

7

The

Lighthouse

Is

Restored

When the light was extinguished in the Cape Hatteras lighthouse in 1936, a substitute light was placed on a skeleton tower further inshore near Buxton Woods. The new structure was a functional replacement for the brick lighthouse but had none of its aesthetic appeal. Resembling some overgrown insect, it stood on spindly legs to peer over the trees and dunes like a mechanical Cyclops.

Residents of the Banks were not pleased with the substitute lighthouse, and efforts to reverse the effects of erosion near the forsaken older beacon continued with renewed fervor. W. E. Byrum and a crew of CCC workers built long windrows of tree

Skeleton steel light tower. From 1936 until 1950, this framework of steel girders was used as a replacement for the Cape Hatteras lighthouse. Situated near the town of Buxton, it was topped by a beacon similar to those used at airports. (Courtesy of the U.S. National Park Service)

branches between the lighthouse and the sea and planted trees nearby. Byrum's concerted efforts on behalf of the lighthouse earned him the affection of the residents, and he became known locally as "Dad" Byrum.

The Park Service continued its campaign to have the region declared a protected zone, preserved in its natural state for tourists who crossed Oregon and Ocracoke inlets by ferry to visit the historic site. In 1937 the service made a formal recommendation for the establishment of a national seashore recreational area for the Outer Banks at Cape Hatteras, and within the year Congress passed a bill establishing the Cape Hatteras National Seashore. It was a historic act, for this was America's first national seashore and one of ten national seashore parks that would be authorized within the next forty years.

The park was now official, but it was far from real. Legal constraints prevented the federal government from purchasing land for the park, and acquisition of the land depended on contributions from benefactors like those who had donated the thousand acres around the lighthouse. North Carolina took a hand in the project by appointing the North Carolina Cape Hatteras Seashore Commission, whose principal task was to acquire title to the needed land. In the same year that the national seashore was established, the National Park Service renovated the double keepers' quarters and repainted the lighthouse inside and out. By 1940 many miles of dunes had been built, and the progress made in reclaiming the Banks was encouraging, but the evolution of the Outer Banks region into a tourist attraction was halted by the onset of World War II, and for five years erosion control was forgotten.

Once again German U-boats traveled across the Atlantic to lie in wait for passing ships off the shores of North Carolina. Lessons forgotten or never learned during World War I were brought home with terrible results during the first few months of 1942. Before residents learned to black out lights in the small villages of the Outer Banks, German captains were able to blast ships as they passed Cape Hatteras at night and were silhouetted against the bright background. From January through June in that first year of the war, so many ships were torpedoed and lost that the area was given the new, grim label of Torpedo Junction to add to its other alias as the Graveyard of the Atlantic. From necessity, America made rapid advances in antisubmarine warfare tactics. Soon the German submarines were sent to join their victims and the countless other wrecks lining the ocean bottom at Diamond Shoals. Much of the wartime action took place within view of the Cape Hatteras lighthouse, but the old brick tower stood empty and dark. Its only function during the war was to serve as a lookout tower.

While the war was still in progress, oil company geologists appeared on the Outer Banks. They suspected that pools of oil might lie under the surface, and their search inflamed the residents with dreams of possible sudden wealth. When the oil companies began buying mineral rights and drilling test holes, dreams of a seashore park were suddenly pushed into the background in favor of a quest for riches. Former support for the park dissipated rapidly and was replaced by vehement resistance to the idea. But when the petroleum engineers packed their gear and abandoned the dry holes they had produced, they left behind much bitterness. For years there was little resurgence of endorsement for the park.

Light Returns to the Lighthouse

As the years passed, the barber-pole-striped lighthouse stood inoperative, but hope had not diminished among Hatteras residents that the light would be restored. In 1946 a shipwreck nine miles north of Cape Hatteras evolved into a renewed effort to return the light to the old lighthouse. The $170,000 yacht *Nautilus* was headed south on a November day so clear that Captain Cadwallader easily spotted the bold stripes of the old lighthouse. Unaware that the lighthouse had been replaced by a steel tower two miles away, he set his course by the old landmark, and when night fell he assumed the flashing signal was from the tower he had seen earlier. As a result of the conflicting sightings, his craft grounded and was demolished in the breakers.

Cadwallader's complaints reached the Coast Guard, and after two years that service decided to investigate the feasibility of restoring the light to the old tower. When it was discovered that the sand stabilization progress credited to the work of "Dad" Byrum had left the old lighthouse one thousand feet from the high tide line, negotiations were started with the Park Service to allow the Coast Guard to use the tower again.

After several months of discussion, the two parties reached an agreement in December 1948 that permitted the Park Service to retain title to the lighthouse but granted the Coast Guard a use-lease for twenty years with an option to renew at the end of that time. The Park Service arranged for removal of the old Fresnel lens, which had been mutilated beyond repair by souvenir hunters, and all agreed that the tower would be preserved in its original form except for necessary repairs. Rust had damaged the metal balcony during the years of neglect, and several of the plate-glass windows had been broken. Wasps buzzed in and out of the damaged cupola, and moisture had left the interior musty and dingy. Countless tourists had scrawled their names like spidery hieroglyphs on every accessible bit of wall. A collage of broken glass and mortar fragments decorated the floor as well as the landings along the corroded spiral stairway.

To prevent further damage until restoration could begin, the Coast Guard replaced the broken doors that dangled on rusty hinges and locked them to prevent unauthorized entry. During the next year, the interior was repainted, windows replaced, and metalwork scraped and painted. White and black stripes spiraled upward around the exterior in a gleaming new coat. Electrical wiring was installed to provide power for a new lantern.

Electric lighting had evolved considerably since 1934, and when the original lamp was found to be inoperable, it was necessary to replace it with an electric beacon. A forty-inch light with a 1,400-watt bulb was installed, and on 23 January 1950 the lighthouse was restored to full operation. The new lamp produced a beam of 250,000 candlepower and was so powerful that it could be seen for twenty miles under clear conditions. The light rotated once every fifteen seconds and provided a visible flash every seven-and-a-half seconds. The lamp's rotation was controlled by a Swiss-made astronomical timer, and it operated on commercially produced electricity. An emergency generator was kept in a nearby shed where oil was once stored. A photoelectric cell served as a switch to turn the light on and off. Given this level of automation, only occasional visits by the Coast Guard were required to check on lighthouse operations. For Banks residents, though, the light had come home.

With the return of the light to the lighthouse, interest in the national seashore park rebounded, and when the Avalon Foundation and the Old Dominion Foundation jointly offered $618,000 to buy land for the proposed park, the North Carolina Council of State appropriated matching funds within a week. The catalyst to convert plans into action had been provided, and in 1953 the Cape Hatteras National Seashore became a reality. The park encompassed all of Hatteras and Ocracoke islands, except for the villages, and included the stately old Cape Hatteras lighthouse. Dedication ceremonies took place five years later.

Tourists were attracted to the new national park, and it was made more accessible to visitors when the Herbert C. Bonner Bridge was built to span Oregon Inlet in 1962. The number of vacationers who came to visit the island and the Cape Hatteras lighthouse grew from thousands to more than two million annually.

The width of the beach between the lighthouse and the breakers continued to vary as storms and currents relocated the sand, and the battle to halt encroachment by the sea continued unabated. In 1966, 312,000 cubic yards of sand were pumped onto the beach in front of the lighthouse, but the sand, which

Diamond Shoals light tower. In 1967 a platform similar to a Texas oil rig tower was erected on the Outer Shoal, replacing the lightship anchored there. Its light signals, which flash warnings over a radius of seventeen miles, supplement the powerful beams of the Cape Hatteras lighthouse. (Courtesy of the U.S. National Park Service)

Modern lamp of the Cape Hatteras lighthouse. This large lantern is one of a pair that send a powerful flash rated at 800,000 candlepower for a distance of more than twenty miles. The light's operation is entirely automated and requires only occasional visits by the U.S. Coast Guard. (Photograph by Mike Booher)

came from the sound side of the island, was so fine-grained that the ocean washed it away in short order.

Also in 1967, the Diamond Shoals lightship that had marked the outer shoal for so long was replaced by a modern light station similar in design to a Texas-style oil drilling platform. From its position a dozen miles at sea, the tower's light flashes every two-and-a-half seconds, and it emits a regular radio signal of "DS DS DS" to warn of the proximity of Diamond Shoals. The Cape Hatteras lighthouse continued to flash its own warnings of the shoals and of the threatening seas that crowded around its base.

In 1967 the National Park Service used sandbags, with some success, to fortify the beach near the lighthouse. Because nylon resists decay, many of the bags remained in place for more than twenty years. In 1969 the navy built three groins of reinforced concrete almost in front of the lighthouse, but storms inflicted moderate damage on these, and six years later they had to be reinforced with sheet steel piling. They were not built to protect the lighthouse but rather the navy's LORAN station. Many now believe that these groins, which extended like parallel fences from the beach into the surf, caused the ocean to swirl around the lighthouse with greater force, thus significantly increasing the erosion of beach there.

Another attempt at sand replenishment was made by the National Park Service in 1971. The sand used this time came from the ocean side of the island in hopes that its larger grains would resist being washed away. A total of 200,000 cubic yards was moved from Hatteras Point, and two years later an astounding one-and-a-third million cubic yards of additional sand were shifted from the point to the lighthouse area.

A new double beacon similar to those used at airports was installed in the lantern room in 1972. Each light measured thirty-six inches in diameter and contained a 1,000-watt bulb. In 1982 these were replaced by twenty-four-inch lanterns, each producing 800,000 candlepower, making it more effective than ever.

All the measures taken to defend the lighthouse were still not adequate to halt the advance of the sea, and by 1975 the waves were breaking just 175 feet from the shattered foundation of the original Cape Hatteras lighthouse, 600 feet south of the new tower. By 1978 the waves at high tide were lapping at the ruins of the former lighthouse, and the portent of this was realized when a severe blizzard in March 1980 completely eradicated the last remnants of the old beacon. Hamilton's lighthouse had endured for more than 175 years, but it was finally destroyed by the same sea that now threatened its newer and larger descendant.

8

Save

the

Lighthouse

From 1950 to 1980, the sea nibbled away the beach in front of the Cape Hatteras lighthouse at a rate of only a few feet each year, and in January 1980 at least 150 feet of sand still separated the waves from the foundation of the historic tower. In that year, though, the sand suddenly began to wash away at an unprecedented rate, spurred on by two severe storms, and more than half of the narrow strip vanished within six months. By autumn only a 70-foot margin of safety remained between the lighthouse and the surf, arousing fears of the beacon's imminent collapse. Alarmed at the prospect of seeing the historic monument crumble into a pile of brick and mangled metal, private citizens and government officials across the state joined in a desperate effort to save it.

A groin stretching into the ocean ten yards from the lighthouse was the only barrier left to fend off the encroaching breakers. Chunks of concrete were hastily thrown into the zone between this seawall and the lighthouse in a frantic attempt to slow the erosion. The MTMA Design Group, an association of Raleigh architects, conducted a $25,000 study and offered the National Park Service several alternatives for long-term protection of the monument. One suggestion was to do nothing and let nature take its course, but residents of Hatteras Island refused to consider letting the famous tower topple into the sea. The strong sentimental attachment that many people felt toward this predominant feature of the Hatteras landscape, coupled with its historical significance, prompted an all-out effort to save it. A local organization, the Outer Banks Preservation Association, formed with the purposes of alerting state leaders to the threat facing the tower and of seeking help to prevent its loss. The lighthouse had been rescued once before, and most supporters believed it could be saved again.

The Save the Cape Hatteras Lighthouse Committee

Tight budgets at both the national and state government levels had left the National Park Service woefully short of funds, with only minimal provisions for safeguarding the lighthouse, and private donations seemed to offer the only chance of preventing further encroachment by the sea. In October 1981 James Hunt, Jr., North Carolina's Democratic governor, and Jesse Helms, the state's Republican U.S. Senator, joined forces to cochair a Save the Cape Hatteras Lighthouse Committee. This committee, the brainchild of Linville businessman Hugh Morton, proposed to raise a million dollars for the preservation of the Cape Hatteras lighthouse.

Morton, one of North Carolina's leading promoters, was a friend to both Helms and Hunt, and he knew they would set aside their political differences to save the lighthouse. The governor and the senator, both strongly loyal to North Carolina, readily agreed to cochair the project. Tom Ellis, an experienced fundraiser, worked with Helms, Hunt, and Morton to get the project underway. The campaign to save the lighthouse was ready to begin.

Because it was to function as a branch of the North Carolina Travel Council, the committee was granted tax-deductible status. Contributors of $100 or more were entitled to become a "Keeper of the Light" and to receive a document, signed by Governor Hunt and Senator Helms, certifying that title. Certificates were also awarded to anyone who raised $500 in contributions. The momentum generated by the committee gathered steam rapidly. Several thousand dollars were given by large corporations based in North Carolina. Schoolchildren across the state raised over $20,000 to save the lighthouse. Save the Light bumper stickers and other lighthouse paraphernalia quickly became best-selling items on the coast, and the 1,500 to 2,000 tourists who visited the lighthouse every day became concerned about the possible loss of the century-old beacon. Secretary of the Interior James Watt expressed his support for the project and recommended that the national government get involved.

Meanwhile, Orrin Pilkey, Jr., a coastal geologist based at Duke University, was expressing reservations about any proposed attempts to block the advance of the ocean. Pilkey argued that the barrier islands exist in a natural equilibrium and that interfering with the processes of nature could upset that delicate balance. His views received widespread publicity, causing some, including the National Park Service, to question the methods that might be used by the Save the Cape Hatteras Lighthouse Committee.

At first Morton and his committee had difficulty raising funds because of the public's serious concerns about the damage that might result from the application of uncertain methods to save the lighthouse. Fearing the potentially destructive effects on the environment and plagued by serious doubts that any protective measures could ultimately prevent the loss of the tower, many were ready to sacrifice the lighthouse in order to protect the beaches. But after the fund drive began to raise substantial sums of money, providing clear evidence of widespread public sentiment in favor of salvaging the famous landmark, the Park Service became convinced that it should try to prevent the destruction of the lighthouse.

By the end of 1981, Morton and his followers still had only vague notions of how to protect the tower, but once money started accumulating, ideas also began to emerge. It was obvious that some immediate measures had to be taken to thwart the inexorable forward progress of the waves; unless erosion could be halted, the question of long-term solutions would become academic. The committee gave some of its funds to the National Park Service to help pay for adding 150 feet to the length of the steel pilings built there earlier by the U.S. Navy and to place sand-filled nylon bags in the path of the advancing tides.

Plans Emerge for Long-Term Protection

By the summer of 1982, the National Park Service was ready to consider the alternatives suggested by the MTMA Design Group for a lasting solution to the lighthouse problem. One plan involved the construction of four giant breakwaters near the ocean's edge, each of which would cost over $1 million and extend a hundred yards or more into the water. These structures, though, would serve only to slow the rate of erosion and carried the added disadvantage of severely restricting swimming and boating over a large area.

Another scheme involved the old technique of sand replenishment. Previous experience with pumping in sand to restore the beach in front of the lighthouse had shown it to be a

Former President Ronald Reagan. The Save the Cape Hatteras Lighthouse campaign gained national recognition when Reagan endorsed the effort. He became an honorary "Keeper of the Light" in November 1981. (Official White House photograph; courtesy of Hugh Morton)

temporary solution at best, and although the estimated cost of the process was only $3 million, an additional $1 million a year might be required to replace the sand as it washed away. A third option was to restore the three jetties built by the navy in 1969 and to construct a fourth to supplement their effect. Many still believed that jetties exacerbated beach erosion, and when the cost was estimated at $16 million plus an additional million every dozen years or so, this plan was deemed unacceptable.

Moving the lighthouse away from danger was yet another alternative. In 1978 the MTMA Design Group had studied the Cape Lookout lighthouse and suggested that it might be preserved if it were dismantled into sections, moved away from the beach, and reassembled. The group now suggested relocating the Cape Hatteras lighthouse by lifting the entire building off its foundations and moving it along tracks laid across the sand. They estimated the cost of such a venture at $3 to $5 million. At a conference held on Hatteras Island in the spring of 1982 to study the alternative plans, some of those attending confused the 1978 Cape Lookout proposal with the 1980 plan for Cape Hatteras and ridiculed the idea of taking the Cape Hatteras lighthouse apart and reassembling it. As a result the conference participants decided that the cost estimates were much too low, and the scheme was rejected without careful examination. David C. Fischetti, a structural engineer from Cary, North Carolina, who had helped develop the plan to move the lighthouse, was distressed that the plan had been misinterpreted, and he began to contact government officials to see if anything could be done.

Finally, in July 1982, the National Park Service accepted a plan to build a basal revetment or seawall around the lighthouse. The wall, to be constructed of concrete and steel, would be octagonal like the base of the light. It would reach twenty-three feet above sea level to surround the lighthouse and would extend another sixteen feet below the surface of the ocean. Its one-foot-thick walls would be reinforced by a twelve-foot-thick riprap of boulders and five-ton concrete pods reaching out like

Artist's conception of a seawall surrounding the Cape Hatteras lighthouse. One plan considered for saving the lighthouse involved the construction of an octagonal revetment around the base. Eventually, if sea levels continued to rise, the seawall would have formed an island with the lighthouse in the center. This plan was later rejected in favor of a scheme to move the lighthouse farther inland. (*Courtesy of the* Raleigh News and Observer)

a talus slope fifty feet from the base. A walkway for visitors would encircle the top of the seawall. The U.S. Army Corps of Engineers developed this seawall plan with the idea that the original construction would enclose three-fourths of the lighthouse base on the sides facing the ocean; if the sea continued to advance, the last quarter of the wall would be built, forming a complete octagon around the tower. Depending on how high the water rose, the seawall eventually might form a small island with the lighthouse standing in the center. The approximate cost of the revetment was set at $5.5 million for the first part of the construction and an additional $2 or $3 million should it later become necessary to completely surround the lighthouse.

The goal of $1 million set by the Save the Cape Hatteras Lighthouse Committee was clearly not sufficient to build the seawall. Support had been promised by the Department of the Interior, giving hope that federal funds would defray the costs of constructing the revetment, but any government help of that magnitude was likely years away. Morton believed the money already raised by the committee could save the lighthouse until other funds became available.

Pilkey was not won over by the arguments for a revetment, even though it was not viewed as an environmental threat. He pointed out that wave energy in the vicinity of the lighthouse is so great the revetment could ultimately become as vulnerable to the combination of wave action, erosion, and storms as the tower it was designed to protect. The Army Corps of Engineers decided to consider other options while a study was undertaken to see if a seawall was a workable solution.

By 1982 legislation had been passed that prevented the federal government from doing anything to protect structures in national seashore areas, and in North Carolina it was already illegal for the state to harden any shoreline. The seawall was viewed by many people as a violation of these principles, and they feared that if action of this type were taken to protect the lighthouse, it might open the way to governmental obligations to protect private beachfront property as well.

In the meantime, while the search for a long-term solution continued, temporary measures were necessary to fend off the sea. Ever present was the threat that one of the sudden storms that frequently swept Hatteras Island could destroy the beacon before a revetment or other scheme for extended protection could be put into place.

The spring of 1981 saw a new and unusual attempt to rebuild the beach around the lighthouse. A retired engineer began to install a type of artificial seaweed called Seascape in the waters at Cape Hatteras. William L. Garrett of Delaware had used his patented device to restore sandy reefs at several other beaches, and when he read about the problems at Hatteras, he was anxious to test his product. The Outer Banks Preservation Society helped him obtain permission to try his invention at Cape Hatteras.

Seascape was designed to imitate the sand-trapping characteristics of natural seaweed. It consisted of plastic tubes covered with four-foot fronds that looked like the appendages on a millipede. The devices, which were manufactured in Roanoke Rapids, North Carolina, were anchored by filling the base tubes with seventy-five pounds of sand or rocks. Some scoffed at the idea, for the unusually powerful waves at Cape Hatteras made it doubtful whether the synthetic seaweed could remain in place long enough for sand to accumulate around it, but Garrett had faith in his invention and donated the first five hundred units. Within eighteen months of their installation, sand had accumulated noticeably behind the Seascape units. Many observers were elated over the results and felt that the potential of the design had been confirmed.

Others were still skeptical. When divers were sent to check on the artificial seaweed, they discovered many of the units buried beneath the sand and others lying uselessly on the beach. So it was difficult to determine whether the accreted sand was caused by Garrett's innovation or was merely the result of natural forces. But there was no doubt that the beach in front of the lighthouse *had* expanded, and the Save the Cape Hatteras Lighthouse Committee decided to invest $165,000 in an additional 5,000 units of Seascape. The committee also paid $10,000 for sandbags to supplement the artificial seaweed. By now almost $300,000 had been raised by the group, and that money went to help the National Park Service preserve the lighthouse until federal funds were available for a long-term option.

Arguments over the effectiveness of the Seascape units persisted. This divisiveness between the leaders of the Save the Cape Hatteras Lighthouse Committee, who believed in the effectiveness of Seascape, and some coastal geologists including Orrin Pilkey, who considered the artificial seaweed useless, expanded as the discussion continued, and the debates were often heated. The accumulation of sand on the beach, whatever the cause, gave time for further study and continued debate; it also, unfortunately, provided an excuse to stall a final decision. Once the urgent need for immediate action was alleviated, the motivation to make permanent arrangements was likewise reduced, although some experts continued to warn that a sudden storm or hurricane could destroy the lighthouse.

The Move the Lighthouse Committee

In 1983 the Army Corps of Engineers announced plans for a riprap zone to protect the south groin and simultaneously began a study of the projected seawall. One year later the riprap was in place, and wave tank experiments were in progress to test the design of the proposed revetment.

While the seawall design was being tested, Orrin Pilkey was invited to speak at a meeting of civil engineers in Raleigh, and there he met David Fischetti. Together they discussed mutual concerns about the welfare of the Cape Hatteras lighthouse and the proposed construction of the revetment. Out of their combined knowledge of coastal geology and structural engineering grew an understanding of the long-term threats to the beacon. Both men were sure the seawall would leave the tower exposed to eventual destruction from winds and storm tides generated by the powerful hurricanes that strike the Banks with unpredictable frequency. Their belief was supported by statements from a weather scientist who had made the same prediction in 1982. Fischetti's knowledge of architectural design and his familiarity with projects that had proven the feasibility of moving large structures convinced him that the lighthouse could be moved out of danger without the necessity or expense of dismantling it. Pilkey, who until then had been ready to sacrifice the lighthouse, began to hope it could be saved without damaging the fragile environment on the Outer Banks.

One year later Fischetti and David Bush, a Duke University

colleague of Dr. Pilkey, were invited to present their scheme for saving the lighthouse to the 1985 Youth Legislative Assembly in Raleigh. Public awareness of the plan grew as newspapers throughout the state included stories about moving the lighthouse. Fischetti wrote letters to U.S. Senators Jesse Helms and Terry Sanford, to the director of the Office of Coastal Management, and to engineers and scientists in several states, expressing his concerns for the lighthouse and presenting the arguments for relocation. Marine geologists, architects, and construction engineers from across the United States wrote to express their support, and two hundred of them banded together to form a Move the Lighthouse Committee, which was officially organized in April 1986. All the scientists and engineers who joined were firmly persuaded that the only way to save the historic Cape Hatteras lighthouse was to move it to higher ground, out of harm's way.

Once formed, the committee began a campaign to stall the construction of the seawall and to persuade the National Park Service to reconsider relocation as a means of saving the lighthouse. In the meantime, though, the final specifications for the seawall were completed, and the Park Service was prepared to begin construction as soon as federal funding could be obtained. It was estimated that the structure could be completed within twenty months, ensuring permanent protection for the lighthouse by 1988. To help prevent damage to the tower before the seawall was finished, the Save the Cape Hatteras Lighthouse Committee funded the installation of an additional 2,700 units of Seascape in August 1986.

Around this time the National Park Service raised questions about the condition of the lighthouse. At over 116 years of age, was it still sturdy and likely to endure? In November 1985 a scaffold was built around the tower so that engineers could examine it for signs of deterioration. The Park Service, at a cost of nearly $200,000, conducted a study to assess weak spots in the brick-and-iron structure and to provide suggestions for remedying any deficiencies. Some of the weaknesses were easy to spot, for storms, wind, lightning, and sun had staged a united assault on the giant tower through the years, creating long crevices in the walls and flaws in the metalwork. Obvious cracks in the balcony had caused the Park Service to restrict public access to that part of the lighthouse in 1976. Visitors who climbed the 268 steps to the top felt uneasy as they noticed the fissures that ran in erratic paths up and down the brickwork. When a large chunk of the tower weighing close to fifty pounds came crashing to earth in 1984, the interior of the building was closed to the public.

As part of a thorough examination of the lighthouse by the National Park Service, metal from the steps, windows, and other iron parts were removed for careful inspection. Core samples were taken from the massive pine beams that still rested beneath the foundation of the lighthouse, and a laser was used to determine the amount of sway to which the tower was subjected by the pressures of wind and sun.

Housbrouck Hunderman Architects and Wiss, Janney, Elstner Associates of Illinois conducted the study. In their report, they asserted that the brick and mortar joints were in excellent condition, that the joints between bricks were still filled solidly throughout the walls, and that the mortar was hard to remove. The vice president of the Brick Institute in Virginia tested the bricks in the lighthouse and declared that they were in excellent shape for their age. These findings added support to the claims of the Move the Lighthouse Committee that the lighthouse could be moved without significant danger to the structure.

The mass of the part of the lighthouse to be moved was estimated at approximately 4,400 tons. Examination of the original plans for the lighthouse, and correlation of the wall design with the total mass, showed that the center of gravity was located only one-third of the way up from the base, providing a stable shape with extreme resistance to toppling. After all, the lighthouse had been built to stand without support against hurricane winds of 150 mph.

Scaffolding surrounds the Cape Hatteras lighthouse. In 1985 the National Park Service undertook a study of the condition of the lighthouse. The structure of the tower was thoroughly checked. Samples of the walls, the foundation, and the metalwork were analyzed for deterioration or weakness. The lighthouse was found to be in excellent shape, and any damage found was scheduled for repairs beginning in 1990. (Photograph by Mike Booher)

By 1987 the federal government had allocated the $5.7 million needed to build the seawall, but the arguments of the Move the Lighthouse Committee were gathering strength, and the president of the National Wildlife Federation in Washington, D.C., added his support to the plan for relocation. The committee pointed out the disturbing finding that the quantity of fresh water needed to mix the concrete for the seawall could drain the underground supplies at Cape Hatteras so severely that saltwater intrusion could result, ruining the wells on the island and causing disaster for the residents.

By May the Park Service was ready to seek bids for construction of the seawall, but the arguments of the Move the Lighthouse Committee were persuasive, and action was postponed until the relocation plan could be reexamined. Some who had originally supported the seawall were now in favor of moving the lighthouse, especially after studies by engineers demonstrated the feasibility and cost-effectiveness of the plan.

The LaPlant-Adair Company of Florida made a visit to the site and submitted a proposal for moving the ancient structure. Among the buildings LaPlant-Adair had already moved were a four-story hospital and an entire football stadium. David Fischetti, who chaired the Move the Lighthouse Committee, pointed out that the Church of the Ascension in Czechoslovakia had been moved successfully in 1975 even though it weighed 12,000 tons, was made of fragile sandstone, contained stained-glass windows, and was maneuvered through two significant turns. Fischetti felt that the major obstacle would be obtaining a decision by the Department of the Interior, and that moving the bureaucracy would be harder than moving the lighthouse.

The proponents of a seawall were equally positive that surrounding the lighthouse with a revetment was the only logical way to protect it, and they argued bitterly against attempts to relocate the old beacon. Many Hatteras residents were opposed to moving the tower from its original location, for two reasons. They believed that the aged tower was too fragile to endure the move and might be damaged or destroyed in the process. They

Artist's rendition of an early plan to move the Cape Hatteras lighthouse. Engineers planned to lift the structure on hydraulic jacks, insert needle beams, and transport the tower on rails to a safer location five hundred feet from its present position. In December 1989 the National Park Service decided that moving the lighthouse was indeed the most likely way to save it. (Courtesy of the Raleigh News and Observer)

also complained that removing the beacon from its original location would diminish its meaning as well as its authenticity as a historical monument. Hugh Morton declared that it was akin to moving the London Bridge to Arizona, where it was deprived of its traditional significance and where even its original name was now of questionable legitimacy. He also worried that moving the aged structure might cause its destruction.

On the other hand, those in favor of relocation cited numerous examples of successful transportation of large, delicate structures, including some American lighthouses, using modern engineering techniques. They also contended that the lighthouse could be moved at a fraction of the cost of building a seawall, and that if it could be moved once, it could, if necessary, be moved again in another hundred years. They were sure the seawall could not protect it for even half a century, as their document "Move It or Lose It" substantiated. They offered a compelling argument that it was better to have the lighthouse in a different location than not to have it at all.

Relying on space-age technology and the strength of the radial brick masonry used by the original builders of the lighthouse, the Move the Lighthouse Committee was confident that the lighthouse could be moved along a direct path to the southwest, coming to rest at a safe distance from the sea. They estimated that the move would take no more than four months.

Those who fought the proposal to relocate the lighthouse were not so sure. They feared the cracks in the brickwork and the age of the tower might cause it to collapse under the stress of tugging it over the sandy ground.

Seeking a Decision

Torn between the two proposals for saving the lighthouse, the National Park Service decided to turn the decision over to the National Academy of Sciences (NAS) in Washington, D.C., a group that could provide a scientific evaluation of the two ideas and render an unbiased decision. When the academy released a preliminary report on 15 October 1987, the initial conclusion was that relocation offered the cheapest and safest way to save the beacon.

The Park Service immediately began preparations for transporting the lighthouse, although a final decision would not come until the following spring. Inclined to concur with the NAS's early opinion that retreat from the sea posed less threat to the safety of the lighthouse than efforts to fight the inexorable encroachment of the sea, the Park Service decided that even if the final decision supported building a seawall, nothing would be lost by strengthening the tower. On the other hand, if the verdict was in favor of relocation, valuable time would be saved by having completed some of the preparations in advance.

In April 1988 the NAS's National Research Council Committee on Options for Preserving the Cape Hatteras Lighthouse reported its conclusions after exhaustive study of the alternatives. Moving the lighthouse was deemed to be not only more economical, but a surer way of protecting it from destruction. The committee estimated the costs of relocation at $4.5 million, versus $6 million for the seawall. Even more significant were the continuing costs of maintaining the seawall, as well as the possibility that the seawall would eventually have to be extended so as to completely enclose the area around the lighthouse. These additions would cost more millions of dollars and offered less hope for enduring protection than relocation.

Countering the arguments that moving the lighthouse would destroy some of its authenticity and change its character, the committee's report pointed out that building a seawall around the tower would not only isolate the lighthouse from the keepers' quarters and other outbuildings, but it would seriously obstruct the view of the beacon from the ground—hardly leaving it in original condition. It also would eliminate any chance of moving the lighthouse in the future.

Even after the NAS's decision was rendered, debate continued between the two factions. The prospective loss of several acres of precious maritime forest was cited as another negative result of any attempt to move the lighthouse, and many partisans continued to advocate fortifying the beaches through additional groins, sand replacement, and the building of a seawall.

By 1989 the National Park Service still had made no effort to pursue either the seawall plan or the relocation proposal, angering those on both sides of the continuing debate. The Park Service was in a dilemma, for no matter which alternative it chose, the decision would alienate supporters of the other plan. More than eight years had elapsed since the MTMA Design Group had first suggested moving the lighthouse, so David Fischetti and the other scientists and engineers of the Move the Lighthouse Committee were no less frustrated and apprehensive than Hugh Morton, who had seen a decade pass since his Save the Lighthouse Committee raised several hundred thousand dollars to support the lighthouse preservation efforts.

Finally, in the late fall of 1989, the National Park Service decided that the lighthouse must be moved if it was to be rescued from destruction. The Move the Lighthouse Committee began to celebrate, while many Hatteras residents and members of the Save the Lighthouse Committee bemoaned the decision. There was a catch to the Park Service's ruling, however. No date was set for the movement, and no funds were designated to pay for it. To those who supported relocation, this meant more disappointment and delay. For those who fought the movement, it meant at least a brief reprieve.

David Bush, a research associate for the Duke University Program for the Study of Developed Shorelines, believed that the lighthouse was already in imminent danger and that too long a delay could be disastrous. He stated that there was a grave risk that any major storm could undercut the structure and cause it to fall. Hurricanes and nor'easters are common along the Outer Banks and have a history of causing severe beach erosion that, in the case of the lighthouse, could be catastrophic.

In the summer of 1990, the Park Service made efforts to protect the lighthouse from the effects of further beach loss by increasing the sandbag revetment around the base of the tower. Several hundred three-ton sandbags were installed by the Carter Construction Company of Hampstead, North Carolina, to increment the tiers of bags placed there in 1983. Some funds for this project were provided by the Save the Lighthouse Committee, which had no qualms about helping shore up the beach area but refused any assistance in efforts toward the tower's relocation.

Few realized that it would be almost another ten years before relocation of the lighthouse would finally be funded. Even fewer might have wagered that it would still be standing, despite several hurricanes and other storms that battered Hatteras Island in the interim. However, the National Park Service was not inactive during this period, spending more than three million dollars to protect the lighthouse from the incursions of the sea as well as restoring its metalwork and strengthening the brick and mortar walls in anticipation of its eventual relocation.

The federal budget fell on hard times during the early 1990s, and no funds were designated by Congress for the relocation of the famous beacon. The National Park Service, which had responsibility for protecting the Cape Hatteras lighthouse, began to seek other alternatives to defend the historic monument. One proposal involved spending nearly two million dollars to build a fourth groin just south of the tower's foundation, in hopes that the new structure might capture enough sand to extend the beach in front of the lighthouse. This plan was stymied by the North Carolina Resources Commission, which declared it to be in violation of a North Carolina law that forbade hardening of the shoreline. Some supporters might have liked to see an exception allowed in this instance, not only for the sake of the lighthouse, but also because it could have opened a loophole to allow protection of other endangered property along the state's coast. Because the use of groins to capture sand in one area can starve and deplete beaches farther down the coast, it is clearly a method that can benefit one area at the expense of another and is thus illegal in the state.

As the years passed, storms came and went, and the lighthouse endured. Nevertheless, the beacon was in a perilous spot, and many worried for its future. In 1998 Hurricane Bonnie hurled towering waves against the Hatteras shore, and water surrounded the base of the lighthouse, causing increased concern for its safety. Hurricanes Bertha and Fran had raked across North Carolina two years earlier, leading some to predict a new pattern in the paths of hurricanes that could increase the threat to the state and to the lighthouse.

Emotions ran high in the continuing controversy, leading Senator Marc Basnight of Dare County, president pro tempore of the North Carolina General Assembly, to call for an ad hoc committee to reexamine the evidence for and against relocating the lighthouse. If the move was to take place, everyone should know that all avenues had been explored thoroughly, and, since the ad hoc committee was composed of faculty from North Carolina State University in Raleigh, whatever decision was reached would not be one offered only by outsiders. This, at least, should make the final choice more palatable to the state's citizenry, whatever their stance on the controversy.

After careful study of the National Research Council's report as well as the massive "Comprehensive Structural Analysis Report" completed in 1988 by Housbrouck Hunderman Architects and the engineering firm of Wiss, Janney, Elstner Associates, both of Illinois, the ad hoc committee agreed that the only way to save the lighthouse was to move it. Committee members cited the additional danger of imminent decay of the timber foundation under the lighthouse if a seawall were built. Only submergence in fresh water for more than a century had kept the timbers intact, and a seawall would likely allow seepage of seawater that would lead to the destruction of the foundation, putting the lighthouse in serious danger of collapse. The committee's report in the fall of 1997 encouraged the National Park

Service to step up its pleas for the federal funding necessary to get the lighthouse move under way.

Armed with the report from the North Carolina study group and the recommendations of the National Academy of Sciences, the Park Service finally was able to generate the momentum it needed. By fiscal year 1998, Congress had appropriated two million dollars to initiate the long-awaited enterprise of saving the lighthouse. This amount would cover the costs of planning and would allow the Park Service to send out a request for bids on the final project. With the assurance that the remainder of the necessary funds would be forthcoming, the Park Service contracted with International Chimney Corporation of Buffalo, New York, in July 1998 to take charge of the project of relocating the Cape Hatteras lighthouse.

In 1999 President Clinton asked Congress to allocate the rest of the money needed to move the historic lighthouse from its precarious position. In the eleven years since the debate had begun, the costs had increased almost threefold over the original estimate, and Congress now appropriated an additional $9.8 million to complete the project. Part of the increase in costs to the now-projected $11.8 million was due to inflation, but monies were also included to pay for restoring the dunes after the lighthouse had been moved, as well as for repositioning the small brick house where oil had been stored, the three water cisterns, and the two dwellings that had served as quarters for the three keepers and their families.

In a last-ditch effort to thwart the relocation effort, Dare County officials sued the National Park Service, but to no avail, and the movers soon arrived. They brought with them an array of the latest equipment in hydraulic transport techniques, some involving technology that had been developed since the NAS had first declared moving the lighthouse to be a feasible operation. Computerized monitoring by space-age instruments would now regulate the move every foot of the way.

Relocation Preparations Begin

Relocation was to be a comprehensive effort in which the lighthouse and its accompanying structures would be transported 2,900 feet across the dunes to a new and safer location 1,600 feet from the sea—almost exactly the distance that had originally separated it from the waves. Preparing the new site for visitors would require the construction of such conveniences as parking spaces and walkways.

The Park Service's own financial and personnel resources were challenged by the immensity of the operation as unexpected expenses developed. Additional help was needed to deal with crowds that varied from more than 10,000 visitors each weekday to twice that number on weekends. Many wanted the chance to witness the historic operation, and the Park Service wanted to assure their safety amid the hazards of the construction site. Tourists were constantly roaming through poison ivy and tick-infested woods to get a better look.

The choice of International Chimney Corporation was a good one, as the company had both the expertise and the experience for such a job. It also had a vested interest in preserving the lighthouse that it had helped refurbish in 1992. While International Chimney had overall responsibility for the relocation effort, however, it was Expert House Movers of Sharptown, Maryland, that would actually move the lighthouse. The two firms had already worked as a team to successfully relocate the Southeast lighthouse at Block Island, Rhode Island, the Cape Cod light at North Truro, Massachusetts, and the Nausett light, also in Massachusetts. Expert House Movers of Chesapeake, Virginia, would move the keepers' quarters and the other structures.

Several other firms, along with a team composed of dozens of technical workers trained in a multitude of engineering, architectural, and environmental fields, would also assist in the process of moving the Cape Hatteras lighthouse. David

Fischetti's DCF Engineering of Cary, North Carolina, was there, along with representatives of a number of other local and out-of-state firms working as advisers, consultants, and project managers. The Illinois firm of Wiss, Janney, Elstner Associates, Quible Associates of Kitty Hawk, Seaboard Surveying and Planning from Kill Devil Hills, North Carolina, Law Engineering and Environmental Services of Georgia, Crum Construction of Buxton, Simone Jaffe Collins from Pennsylvania, Fenner and Proffitt of Wilson, and Schmertmann and Crapps from Florida all played roles in the relocation.

Nothing was to be done without proper care, and every precaution was taken to ensure the safety of the lighthouse. The narrow runway of sand that would serve as the move corridor was graded, graveled, and compacted to support the movement of the precious, 4,400-ton cargo on its half-mile trek. The additional weight of the steel support beams made a total of 4,900 tons that would have to be moved. Part of the route led up a slight incline, and the focal plane of the lighthouse, when it was finally positioned on its new base, would be about two feet higher than before.

First, though, the lighthouse had to be separated from the foundation of crossed timbers on which it had rested for 130 years. Water was pumped from around the timber mat, leaving the granite foundation that reached from about seven feet below ground level to the foot of the tower exposed for cutting. The hard stone was then sliced through by a diamond-edged cable saw, chipped away by pneumatic hammers, and finally removed to allow the insertion of a platform on which the lighthouse would rest for its journey. Shoring towers were placed under the lighthouse as the granite was removed, and a steel mat was positioned atop the original pine timber foundation to prevent the wooden beams from springing upward as the nearly 5,000-ton weight was removed from them.

The platform placed under the lighthouse was formed of double-wide flange steel beams. Steel crossbeams were clamped onto the top of the main beams to create a 60' × 72' platform

Workers remove the granite blocks and rubble from under the lighthouse as it is lifted for relocation. (Photograph by Mike Booher for the National Park Service)

to support the structure. Beneath the main beam assembly, a hundred hydraulic jacks, each with a 100-ton capacity, were positioned to lift the lighthouse above the timber base. The jacks were situated so as to exert their force downward against the foundation to help prevent the distortion of the ancient wood timbers. As the apparatus slowly lifted the lighthouse, ten inches at the time, new oak timbers and metal beams were inserted to hold the now-separated tower in place until the jacks could be reset for another thrust. Careful monitoring of the jacks kept the upward movement smooth and level.

When the tower had been lifted about eight feet, a rolling carriage system was installed beneath it. The keepers' houses had been moved on rubber rollers, but steel would be needed for the massive weight of the lighthouse. After 9,000 pieces of oak cribbing were in place beneath the main beams, the hydraulic jacks that had lifted the lighthouse were repositioned into a three-point system based on the elementary geometric principal that three points determine a plane. It is the same principal employed in the stabilizing properties of a camera tripod. Stability could be maintained by equalizing the force exerted by the hydraulic jacks underneath the lighthouse, keeping it steady throughout its trip.

Roll beams with attached roller dollies were set in place, and five push jacks were installed at the rear to force the whole structure along its way. The push jacks were attached at a slight upward angle so that, as each made its maximum five-foot thrust, the lighthouse moved forward about four feet. An ingenious arrangement of hydraulically controlled clamps allowed the jacks to be disengaged and reattached for the next shove much more quickly than if they had been connected by bolts, thus saving time and accelerating the relocation.

Moving the Lighthouse

At about 3:00 P.M. on Thursday, 17 June 1999, on a dreary day when misting rain left the tower and its supporting apparatus glistening from the dampness, the gradual process of moving the Cape Hatteras lighthouse on its historic journey began. There was no dampening the spirits of those in attendance, and to show the movers' confidence in the safety of their apparatus, Joe Jakubik of International Chimney Corporation stood underneath the lighthouse as it rolled, and Bob Reynolds, superintendent of the National Park Service at Cape Hatteras, rode at the top.

The lighthouse began its move slowly, as if uncertain of its bearings, and by 5:00 P.M. at the end of the first day it had covered only about 10 feet. But its rate of progress gradually increased in the days that followed, finally reaching an average of more than 125 feet per day. The best day saw an advance of nearly 300 feet.

In spite of confidence in their ability to safely ferry the lighthouse to its new site, the contractors worried about the possibility of a storm's interrupting the journey. If a serious blow were to strike the island before the lighthouse had been moved at least 800 feet, there would be few dunes and trees to offer

Hydraulic push jacks are placed at the rear of the platform to propel the lighthouse forward. (Photograph by Mike Booher for the National Park Service)

protection, and the exposed position of the lighthouse could be a serious threat. Getting the move started before the height of hurricane season reduced the danger, but the movers did not breathe easy until they had covered one-third of the total distance and were well inside the protection zone afforded by the maritime forest.

Dozens of sensors placed along the interior and exterior of the lighthouse measured stress, temperature, vibration, and that greatest of all concerns, tilt. Computerized control of these sensors allowed continual monitoring of equilibrium even when no work was in progress. Engineers could even be awakened at night if the computers happened to detect some anomaly in the readings. Yet in the salt-laden, misty air on Hatteras Island, even this elaborate array of instruments was susceptible to false readings. Once, when a small degree of tilt developed, an erroneous correction was indicated, leading to an increase in the tilt instead of its elimination. A surveyor observing a reflector at the top of the lighthouse through a robotic surveying instrument on the ground noticed the discrepancy and reported it so proper leveling could take place. The incident probably posed no danger to the lighthouse, but afterward a large, old-fashioned plumb bob was suspended inside the structure to provide additional backup for electronic detectors should the lighthouse show any tendency to sway.

The steady progress of the move might have occurred at a faster pace had it not been for the need to reuse the rails over which the lighthouse traveled. Each section of beams had to be picked up and relocated to the front of the track as it was passed over in transit, in an action resembling a leapfrog process. The movers were careful to stagger the replacement of the beams so that the ends were not all flush, lest a straight joint line be created that might have produced cumulative structural weakness.

The move was made more economical by the use of steel girders from earlier lighthouse relocations. Also, the movers continually scooped up and reused the gravel from the rail beds as the tower moved forward; this same gravel would be used again by the National Park Service in its later efforts to restore the area.

As the lighthouse progressed, the initial, tentative creep at a barely perceptible one inch per minute gradually quickened as soap was rubbed on the rails to reduce friction. The beacon was soon gliding along at a pace easily detectable by the naked eye, and one no longer had to chart its position against the backdrop of trees from day to day to confirm that it was actually being moved. This visible evidence sparked a new awareness that the historic event was really taking place.

The last few feet were covered slowly, but finally, at 1:23 P.M. on 9 July 1999, the little strip of blue tape that marked the journey's end was reached by the leading edge of the tower. A trip that was originally estimated to take up to six weeks had been completed in just three. The Cape Hatteras lighthouse stood majestically above a new sixty-foot-square concrete pad. That four-foot-thick foundation would hold it for perhaps the next 130 years.

Steel roller beams serve as tracks to bear the massive weight of the lighthouse along the move corridor. (Photograph by Mike Booher for the National Park Service)

Safe at Last

The movement of the lighthouse attracted hundreds of thousands of visitors to the Outer Banks to watch the historic transfer of the beacon to safe ground. Even those who had fought the plan could breathe a sigh of relief that the objective had been achieved safely. Those who championed movement as the right way to save the venerable lighthouse had seen their convictions corroborated and their trust in modern engineering affirmed. The skilled and dedicated men and women who had caused it to happen could be proud of their accomplishment. Despite many warnings of possible disasters, the lighthouse had endured the transition to its new location without harm.

Barely had the beacon reached its new location when Hurricane Dennis crashed into the Outer Banks. Bearing winds of 130 miles per hour, the storm drove towering waves against Hatteras Island, slicing the slender barrier island from ocean to sound in one location and isolating the town of Buxton. One window of the lighthouse was blown out by the storm, and a temporary weather station at the top of the tower was destroyed. But even though the lighthouse had not yet been secured to its new foundation, it suffered little other damage. The powerful surf washed to within two dozen feet of the original foundation. One can only guess whether the lighthouse would have been damaged had it remained there, but the ominous prospect of danger from future hurricanes cannot be ignored.

Some still lament the displacement of the famed lighthouse from its original site, but speculation over whether it should have been left alone is now fruitless, and questions about its chances of survival at its former location have become moot. The movement of the Cape Hatteras lighthouse was a unique and historic event. It was a phenomenal performance and a credit to the engineers and contractors who accomplished it. No matter what one thinks of the decision to make the move, the final result is that the lighthouse still stands as a memorial to the men who built it and a proud symbol of the maritime history of the state and nation to which it belongs.

Epilogue

Since 1870 the Cape Hatteras lighthouse has stood on North Carolina's Outer Banks warning sailors of the dangers of Diamond Shoals. The current structure is the second of two lighthouses built at the edge of the sea near the stormy point of Cape Hatteras. It was a nineteenth-century replacement for the inadequate sandstone tower raised there seventy years earlier in a futile attempt to warn ships away from the menacing underwater dunes that, with the aid of capricious winds and shifting sands, snared ships mercilessly from the nearby shipping lanes. This deadly zone, nicknamed the Graveyard of the Atlantic, formed a cauldron of intersecting warm and cold currents within which stranded ships were quickly pounded to bits by the waves and where castaways had little hope of rescue.

Continuing heavy losses of both ships and lives dictated changes to the first lighthouse and eventually led to the construction of its larger and more powerful replacement. First lit near year's end in 1870, the new brick-and-iron lighthouse was an amazing example of architecture and craftsmanship. With its height and its candy-striped pattern of alternating black and white bands that spiraled upward from the base, the beacon stood out boldly from its background and was easily recognizable from land or sea.

Complementing the lighthouse's unusual height was a powerful lantern with a first-order Fresnel lens; together, the two features enabled the beacon to produce an extraordinarily effective signal to warn ships away from disaster. Well known, respected, and revered by sailors from all over the world, the tower on Hatteras also became one of the most popular lighthouses in America. When rising sea levels threatened the famous structure late in the twentieth century, it was only natural that many people wanted to rescue it from disaster.

The debate over how best to save it was lively, but scientific study indicated that the tower must be moved away from the eroding shoreline, and in the winter of 1998 movers appeared on Hatteras Island to attempt the deliverance of the lighthouse. By the spring of 1999 the lantern was extinguished as all the parties involved readied themselves for the undertaking. The move progressed faster than anticipated, and within three weeks of the first nudge away from its original site, the lighthouse was sitting safely atop a new concrete base only a half-mile from the place Dexter Stetson had selected.

On 13 November 1999, the lamp was relit after a rare eight-month hiatus in its operation. For two-thirds of a year, the familiar flash of the lantern had not been seen in the dangerous waters around Diamond Shoals. Yet, during that time, many eyes on Hatteras Island, throughout the state, and across America were on the darkened tower, for its continued existence would remain under threat until the plans of the engineers who sought to guarantee its future had been safely accomplished.

Witnessing the lighthouse's move was a sad experience for many who were used to seeing the beacon in the familiar location it had occupied all their lives. Some doubters harbored grave concerns about the ability of the beloved monument to withstand the rigors of the journey. But even those who fought against its relocation must have wished it a safe passage once it was on course to safer ground. Despite the emotional debate that preceded the event, the safe relocation of the lighthouse left neither side the loser, for it ensured that the monument was preserved for present and future generations to enjoy. To have allowed it to fall into the sea would have meant the tragic loss of an important symbol of our heritage.

The teams responsible for moving the lighthouse had confidence in their skills, their equipment, and the integrity of the structure first assembled by Dexter Stetson's crew. They had at their disposal instruments, tools, and machinery undreamed of by that original construction team. Stetson himself could hardly have imagined that the lighthouse his men built from more than a million bricks, along with all its heavy metal, glass, and intricate mechanisms, could ever be picked up, intact, from its bed of timbers and transported to a new site. Even with modern technology, it was still a remarkable feat.

It is perhaps no less remarkable that Dexter Stetson and his crew were able to build a structure of such quality and strength on the edge of a remote, sandy island on the stormy Atlantic coast with nothing but their hands, their ingenuity, and the simplest of tools. In such an isolated location, all supplies had to be delivered by sea, and weather, insects, and sickness posed constant impediments to the builders' progress. The lighthouse owes its present safety not only to the competence of the relocation team, but to the master craftsmen who designed and built it in a bygone century.

The Cape Hatteras light is not the only lighthouse along the Outer Banks of North Carolina that faces threats. Though it is the tallest of the four coastal beacons lining the narrow arc of sand that curves eastward from Virginia to Cape Lookout, three other towers were also important components of the system that allowed ships to navigate the state's coast without losing sight of a lighthouse. These towers, their kinship clearly displayed by the similarity of their designs, include one at Cape Lookout, another at Bodie Island, and the Currituck Beach light at Corolla. Only the Cape Hatteras lighthouse was built so near the shore, but the others are not free of danger.

The switch to automated operation of lighthouses eliminated the resident keepers who had fought a daily battle to maintain the beacons in good order. Divided responsibilities among the U.S. Coast Guard, the National Park Service, and various private groups also has left the responsibility for preservation and upkeep uncertain. In the harsh environment occupied by lighthouses, the corrosive effects of normal weathering are compounded by the persistent winds and salty mists that weaken the metal and mortar composition of the buildings and strip the paint from their exteriors.

Recent agreements between the Coast Guard and the National Park Service have cleared the way for refurbishments of the Cape Lookout and Bodie Island lighthouses. The Cape Lookout lighthouse has been repainted, and restoration work on the Bodie Island tower will be finished by soon after the turn of the century; this work includes making its spiral stairway safe for climbing. A private group has arranged to maintain the Currituck Beach lighthouse, and it remains in good condition, accessible to all who wish to climb to its top.

The Ocracoke lighthouse is a channel light and bears little resemblance to the tall beacons standing to its north and south. It is well-maintained, however, and is still in operation after 175 years—the oldest working lighthouse in the state.

Lighthouses are visible reminders of America's maritime tradition as well as monuments to the nation's historic architecture. That many are still in service as working lights today is a tribute to those who built and maintained them. The rescue of the Cape Hatteras lighthouse has not only saved a beacon, but ensured the future of a symbolic link to a time when seafarers could rely on little more than a compass and their sailing skills to help them cross unmarked seas and navigate the storms and shoals that threatened both their ships and their lives.

No one knows for certain if the oceans will continue to rise, but some pessimists predict that melting glaciers will raise sea levels as much as three feet over the next hundred years. If that happens, the Cape Hatteras lighthouse will no longer be safe even in its new location, but then neither will the Outer Banks themselves, or any of the other structures perched precariously along their shores. For now, though, the lighthouse once again sits as far from danger as it did when it was first built over a century ago. Ultimately, it is a pawn in the struggle between humankind and nature, and only time and technology will determine the victor, but at least a small battle has been won, and the Cape Hatteras lighthouse lantern still shines over the Graveyard of the Atlantic.

Bibliography

Allegood, Jerry, "Debate Rages on Ways to Save the Lighthouse." *Raleigh News and Observer*, 17 May 1989.

———. "Future Erodes for Coastal Post." *Raleigh News and Observer*, 21 May 1989.

———. "Lighthouse Aid Surges as Atlantic Rises." *Raleigh News and Observer*, 3 August 1981.

———. "Paraphernalia on Lighthouse 'Best Sellers' on N.C. Coast." *Raleigh News and Observer*, 3 August 1981.

Bailey, Anthony. *The Outer Banks*. New York: Farrar, Straus and Giroux, 1987, Michael di Capua Books.

Basso, Hamilton, "If Tortugas Let You Pass." *American Heritage*, February 1956.

Beaver, Anthony. *A History of Lighthouses*. Secaucus, N.J.: Citadel Press, 1973.

Booher, Mike. "The Keeper of the Light." *Hatteras Monitor*, October 1989.

Brown, Aycock. "Cape Stormy." *Saturday Evening Post*, 3 August 1940.

Brown, Dick. "Hatteras Lighthouse Last Link to an Era Passed." *Fayetteville Observer*, 20 January 1982.

Burwell, Mrs. M. A. "Shipwreck Off Hatteras, 1812." *North Carolina Booklet* 21 (1922): 90–100.

Chaffee, Allen. *Heroes of the Shoals*. New York: Henry Holt and Company, 1935.

Collier, Barnard L. "Orrin Pilkey on the Beach." *Raleigh News and Observer*, 4 December 1988.

Committee on Options for Preserving Cape Hatteras Lighthouse, National Research Council. *Saving Cape Hatteras Lighthouse from the Sea: Options and Policy Implications*. Washington, D.C.: National Academy Press, 1988.

Conway, Martin R. *The Outer Banks: An Historical Adventure from Kitty Hawk to Ocracoke*. Shepherdstown, W.Va.: Carabelle Books, 1984.

Corey, Cindy. *Exploring the Lighthouses of North Carolina*. Chapel Hill, N.C.: Provincial Press, 1962.

Couch, Ray. "Island Magic, Keepers Quarters Have Long, Rich History." *Outer Banks Current*, 26 May 1983.

Davis, William C., ed. *The Image of War: 1861–1865*. Vol. 3, *The Embattled Confederacy*. New York: Doubleday, 1982.

Dean, Earl. "Tallest Atlantic Coast Lighthouse Tower Is Wrecked by the Hands of Vandals." *Durham Morning Herald*, 14 November 1948.

Dean, G. E. "New Lighthouse Warning Ships Off Cape Hatteras." *Raleigh News and Observer*, 11 October 1936.

DeBlieu, Jan. *Hatteras Journal*. Golden, Colo.: Fulcrum, 1987.

Dew, Joe. "Decision to Move Light Held." *Raleigh News and Observer*, 17 May 1989.

———. "Moving Lighthouse Best Way to Save It, Science Panel Says." *Raleigh News and Observer*, 28 April 1988.

Dumbell, Jim. "Hatteras Lighthouse in Trouble." *Charlotte Observer*, 26 October 1980.

Dunbar, Gary S. *Historical Geography of the North Carolina Outer Banks*. Baton Rouge: Louisiana State University Press, 1958.

Ellis, William S. "Lonely Cape Hatteras, Besieged by the Sea." *National Geographic*, September 1969, pp. 393–421.

Faulkner, Janice Hardison. "The Lighthouse Keeper." *Tar Heel*, February 1980.

Floherty, John J. *Sentries of the Seas*. Philadelphia: J. B. Lippincott, 1942.

Hanson, Dennis. "The Tide Is Turning for Old Beacons Adrift at Land's End." *Smithsonian*, August 1987, pp. 99–108.

Hart, Kathy. "Coastal Beginnings." *Coast Watch*, January 1986, pp. 1–3.

Herndon, Nash. "Lighthouse Projects Fight Effects of Age, Elements of Hatteras." *Raleigh News and Observer*, 17 November 1955.

_____. "Need for Light at Hatteras Seen Early." *Raleigh News and Observer*, 17 November 1985.

Holland, Francis Ross, Jr. *A History of the Cape Hatteras Light Station*. Washington, D.C.: National Park Service, U.S. Department of Interior, 1968.

Jackson, Thomas C., and Diana Reische, eds. *Coast Alert: Scientists Speak Out*. San Francisco, Calif.: Coast Alliance by Friends of the Earth, 1981.

Jones, Abe D., Jr. "Prints on Sale to Save Lighthouse." *Greensboro Daily News and Record*, 12 December 1982.

Kaufman, Wallace, and Orrin Pilkey, Jr. *The Beaches Are Moving*. Durham, N.C.: Duke University Press, 1983.

Lawson, John. *A New Voyage to Carolina*. Chapel Hill: University of North Carolina Press, 1967.

Leonard, Jonathan N. *Atlantic Beaches*. New York: American Wilderness/Time-Life Books, 1972.

Lione, Louise. "Hunt, Helms in Harmony over Save-the-Lighthouse Album." *Charlotte Observer*, 21 September 1984.

Lisle, Lorance D. "Foundation of the Cape Hatteras Lighthouse." *Shore and Beach*, April 1985, pp. 29–31.

McCrary, Elissa. "Lighthouse Is Perched Near Disaster." *Greensboro Daily News*, 11 June 1981.

MacNeill, Ben Dixon. "Coast Guard Padlocks Lighthouse." *Raleigh News and Observer*, 30 January 1949.

_____. *The Hatterasman*. Winston-Salem, N.C.: John F. Blair, 1958.

_____. "Outer Banks Light to Glow Again." *Raleigh News and Observer*, 27 October 1949.

Martin, Terry. "They're Saving the Lighthouse . . . or Are They?" *Winston-Salem Journal*, 19 June 1983.

Meekins, Victor. "Hatteras Banks." *Raleigh News and Observer*, 14 April 1935.

Mitchell, Broadus. *Alexander Hamilton, Youth to Maturity 1755–1788.* New York: Macmillan, 1957.

Monsell, Linda. "NPS Final Word—Move-It We Say 'No'!" *Hatteras Monitor*, June 1989.

Morris, Paul C. *American Sailing Coasters of the North Atlantic.* Chardon, Ohio: Bloch and Osborn Publishing Company, 1973.

Owen, Francis C. *Sentinels of the Sea.* New York: F. A. Owen Publishing Company, 1926.

Powell, Anne Elizabeth. "Back from the Brink." *Civil Engineering,* October 1999.

Rankin, Hugh F. *The Pirates of Colonial North Carolina.* Raleigh: North Carolina Department of Cultural Resources, Division of Archives and History, 1986.

Roberts, Bruce, and Cheryl Shelton-Roberts. *Moving Hatteras: Relocating the Cape Hatteras Light Station to Safety.* Morehead City, N.C.: Lighthouse Publications, 1999.

Schenck, Anne. "The Life Savers." *Tar Heel*, May/June 1978, pp. 34–39.

Schoenbaum, Thomas. *Islands, Capes, and Sounds: The North Carolina Coast.* Winston-Salem, N.C.: John F. Blair, 1982.

Seessel, Adam. "Lighthouse Move Gathers Steam." *Raleigh News and Observer*, 16 October 1987.

Selby, Holly. "The Light of Their Lives." *Raleigh News and Observer*, 21 May 1989.

Shabica, Stephen V. *Shoreline Changes at Cape Hatteras National Seashore 1937–1977.* Washington, D.C.: National Park Service, U.S. Department of Interior, 1978.

Snow, Edward Rowe. *Famous Lighthouses of America.* New York: Cornwall Press, 1955.

Steadman, Tom. "Don't Move Lighthouse, Says Son of Last Keeper." *Raleigh News and Observer*, 17 July 1989.

Stick, David. *Dare County: A History.* Raleigh: North Carolina Department of Cultural Resources, Division of Archives and History, 1970.

———. *Graveyard of the Atlantic.* Chapel Hill: University of North Carolina Press, 1952.

———. *North Carolina Lighthouses.* Raleigh: North Carolina Department of Cultural Resources, Division of Archives and History, 1980.

———. *The Outer Banks of North Carolina, 1584 to 1958.* Chapel Hill: University of North Carolina Press, 1958.

Thompson, Roy. "Hamilton's Nausea Caused Hatteras Light." *Winston-Salem Journal*, 8 July 1965.

———. "Hatteras: How Long the Light?" *Winston-Salem Journal*, 14 December 1980.

Whitehouse, Frank E. "Cape Hatteras Lighthouse: Sentinel of the Atlantic Graveyard." *Regional Review* 3, no. 2 (1939): 11–16.

Williams, Charles T., II. *The Kinnakeeter*. New York: Vantage Press, 1975.

Wolverton, Ruthe, and Walt Wolverton. *The National Seashores*. Kensington, Md.: Woodbine House, 1988.

Yocum, Thomas. "Elected Officials Join Efforts to Save Hatteras." *Lighthouse News*, Fall 1996.

———. "Fate of Lighthouse up to Congress." *Lighthouse News*, Fall 1998.

———. "The Most Famous Moving Job in Lighthouse History Is Starting." *Lighthouse News*, Winter 1998.

———. "Senate Votes Initial Funds for Lighthouse Move." *Lighthouse News*, Fall 1997.

Young, Dianne. "The Jewels of Southern Shores." *Southern Living*, April 1989.

Index

GAYLORD S